SWISS
MONEY
SECRETS

HOW *YOU* CAN

SWISS

LEGALLY HIDE YOUR

MONEY

MONEY IN SWITZERLAND

SECRETS

ADAM STARCHILD

PALADIN PRESS
BOULDER, COLORADO

Also by Adam Starchild:

Keep What You Own
Portable Wealth
Using Offshore Havens for Privacy and Profits

CONTENTS

CHAPTER 1

A BRIEF HISTORY OF MONEY:

AND WHY THIS HISTORY MATTERS TO YOU

The evolution of money has been a long and often difficult process as societies searched for ways to develop reliable and lasting systems of commerce and finance.

Over the course of history, money has changed its physical appearance as people refined its shapes and sizes into convenient and practical forms. At the same time, money's nature has changed. From the days of the Roman gold aureus to the original U.S. silver dollar, money's intrinsic worth—meaning its precious metal content—was a paramount measure of its value. Today, money's value is measured not by its material worth but by what it can buy—its purchasing power.

The long and colorful history of money began when

people in ancient civilizations learned they could trade for things they needed rather than produce them. However, trade was often complicated, with people not able to compare the value of different goods. And finding an appropriate trading partner was difficult—for example, a fisherman couldn't get wheat from a farmer who didn't want fish, and a candlemaker couldn't get bread from a baker who didn't need candles.

As a result, people learned to use prized ornaments or agricultural products as standards by which the values of different things could be compared. From time to time, beads, shells, rocks, fish, hooks, grain, and cattle were used as money.

Most types of early money were made from metal because it was durable and easy to carry. About 2,500 B.C. the Egyptians produced one of the first types of metal money in the form of rings. The Chinese used gold cubes about 400 years later.

The first metal coins were struck in Lydia (now western Turkey) in about 700 B.C. Made from an alloy of gold and silver called electrum, the coins—known as "staters"—were actually bean-shaped pellets stamped by the government with their weight and purity. Because these coins were made of precious metal, they had intrinsic value, meaning that they had value in and of themselves, apart from their official designation as money.

The ancient Greeks also minted coins, which replaced the handfuls of iron spits that they had been using. In fact, the word "drachma"—which is the base unit of currency in Greece today—is a derivative of the Greek word for "handful." A number of numismatic innovations are credited to the Greeks, among them the first coin with designs on both sides, the first series of coins issued in different denominations, the first coin with a human representation (the goddess Athena), and the first commemorative coin (celebrating a military victory). Greek coins were also the first international currency, being widely used in trade throughout the Mediterranean.

Another major development came in about 300 B.C. when the Romans issued their first coin—the "as," which was made of bronze. Traditionally, 100 of these were equal to one cow. In later years, Julius Caesar authorized the minting of the gold aureus, which became one of the most widely used coins in the ancient world for more than 300 years.

Smaller denominations of Roman coins that did not contain gold or silver were struck with "sc," the seal of the Roman Senate, to bolster their acceptability. While these coins had no value in and of themselves, they were widely accepted because of the prestige of the gold aureus. This was one of the first successful examples of the circulation of fiat currency—currency that is valuable because of its purchasing power rather than because of its precious metal content.

This early attempt at using fiat currency failed in the fourth century when the Romans began issuing ever-increasing amounts of fiat coins to compensate for insufficient quantities of gold needed to mint the aureus, which was in demand throughout the empire. Huge budget deficits in the Roman government and a loss of confidence in coins caused catastrophic inflation that eventually destroyed the Roman monetary system.

Ironically, it was during the post-Roman era that the Roman solidus became the most enduring coin in history, circulating throughout Europe and the Near East for more than 700 years. The solidus owes its incredible longevity to its largely unchanged appearance and gold content over time, which helped to maintain public confidence in the coin.

While coins remained the primary medium of exchange for centuries, during the Crusades people sought alternatives as travel become more common and more dangerous. The precursor to European paper money was born in the form of "letters of credit"—promissory notes between two parties that generally could not be cashed by anyone else. The use of these letters was aimed at thwarting highway bandits who wanted coins, not paper, which was impossible for them to cash.

The Europeans were not the first people to discover the advantages of using paper money. Its lineage can be traced back to about 2,500 B.C. to the clay tablets on which the Babylonians wrote bills and receipts. The Tang Dynasty in China issued the first known paper money in 650 A.D., and the earliest piece of currency that exists today—a Chinese 10-kuan note—dates back to this time.

Centuries later, in 1273, Marco Polo reported that the Mongol Emperor Kublai Khan issued mulberry bark paper notes in China bearing his seal and the signature of his treasurers. Marco Polo described the monetary system: "All these pieces of paper are issued with as much solemnity and authority as if they were pure gold and silver . . . and the Khan causes every year to be made such a vast quantity of this money, which costs him nothing, that it must be equal in amount to all the treasure in the world." With an overabundance of fiat currency in circulation, it is not surprising to learn that the Mongol-imposed monetary system suffered terrible inflation. Eventually the Mongols left China.

A major step in the development of paper money took place in 1661 when the Stockholm Banco of Sweden issued the first bank notes, which were private obligations of the bank and could be redeemed there in gold or silver by the bearer. Because redemption in precious metals was guaranteed, many people had enough confidence in the value of the notes to exchange them for goods and services. However, Swedish merchants feared that the notes would be bought up by foreigners who would redeem them and eventually deplete Sweden's gold and silver reserves. The issue lasted only one year.

In the seventeenth century, colonists settling in

North America brought coins with them, but most of these were quickly returned to Europe to pay for goods that were not produced in the colonies. This led to a shortage of coins, so Indian wampum—beads of polished shells strung in strands—was widely used as money throughout the colonies. However, when settlers learned to counterfeit wampum, it lost its value.

In addition to wampum, the colonists also used as money those items that were staples of the local economies because they were always in demand. For example, in Virginia it was tobacco, and in Massachusetts it was grain and fish. Nails and bullets frequently were used for small change.

After trade between the colonies and the West Indies developed, Spanish eight-reales coins circulated widely. These coins, known as "pieces of eight," were used until 1857. They were frequently cut to make change: half a coin was "four bits" and a quarter section was "two bits"—a slang expression for the modern American quarter.

The first coin struck in the colonies was the pine tree shilling—which bore a picture of a pine tree—in a Boston mint in 1652. All issues of the coin, even those struck in later years, declared that no additional coins had been minted since 1652 in case the British Crown decided to enforce its ban on the colonists producing their own coins. Despite the efforts of the colonists, the British shut down the mint in 1686.

During the eighteenth century, again contrary to British wishes, hundreds of different types of paper notes were printed throughout the colonies. Those notes, issued before the American Revolution, usually were denominated in pounds and shillings and made reference to the Crown of England for credibility. Some colonies issued too many bills, however, and their value quickly sank to small fractions of their face amount, making trade between colonies difficult. Despite the depreciation, these bills helped offset economic slumps caused by a scarcity of metallic money in an expanding economy.

Before the start of the American Revolution, the Continental Congress, facing huge expenses without adequate taxing power, authorized a limited issue of currency in 1775—the first paper currency issued by what was to become the United States. These notes, called continentals, were printed from plates engraved by Paul Revere to read "The United Colonies" and sometimes even depicted colonial minutemen. They had no backing in gold or silver and could be redeemed only if and when the colonies became independent.

In January 1776, the Continental Congress made it treasonous for people not to accept continentals or to discourage their circulation in any way. In 1777, after the Declaration of Independence, the first notes bearing "The United States" were issued. However, because people were reluctant to accept paper money, well-known revolutionary figures were asked to sign the notes to give them credibility.

For about a year and a half, continentals changed hands at close to face value, but this stability was short-lived. People hoarded goods and coins during the war, which caused inflation. As a result, continentals became basically worthless. As George Washington commented: "A wagon-load of money will scarcely purchase a wagon-load of provisions." The currency's vanishing value led to the expression for worthlessness that remains today— "not worth a continental."

The failure of continentals produced a deep mistrust of paper money throughout the colonies. However, the brief period when continentals circulated successfully was significant because it marked the first time that the worth of U.S. currency lay in its purchasing power, as it does today, and not in its intrinsic value.

After the failure of continentals, more than 70 years passed before the federal government would issue paper money again. However, until then, state-chartered banks made up for the lack of a national currency by issuing their own paper notes, which were obligations of individual banks. These state-bank notes became the dominant form of currency used between the time of the American Revolution and the Civil War.

Each bank designed its own notes, so they differed in size, color, and appearance. By 1860, an estimated 8,000 different state-banks were circulating what were sometimes called "wildcat" or "broken" bank notes in denominations from $1 to $13.

The nickname wildcat came about because some of the less reputable banks were located in low-population areas and were said to attract more wildcats than customers. People also called the notes broken bank notes because of the frequency with which some of the banks failed, or went broke.

Because these notes had varying degrees of acceptance and were not always redeemable in gold or silver on demand, they often circulated at substantial discounts from face value. These conditions made counterfeiting relatively easy, and bogus notes abounded.

In 1861, in an effort to finance the Civil War, the federal government issued the first paper money since continentals. The demand notes of 1861 were popularly called "greenbacks" because of the color on their reverse side.

In 1862, Congress issued $150 million of legal tender notes, more commonly known as United States notes, and retired the greenbacks. These new notes were the first that were made legal tender for all debts except import duties and interest on the public debt. Confidence in U.S. notes began to decline when the Treasury stopped redeeming them in coins during the Civil War to save gold and silver. However, redemption resumed in 1879.

Even though U.S. notes were generally accepted, most paper currency circulating between the Civil War and World War I consisted of national bank notes. This currency, uniform in size and general appearance, was issued by thousands of banks across the country. The federal government granted charters to these banks under the National Bank Acts of 1863 and 1864, allowing the banks to issue notes using U.S. government securities as backing. From 1863 to 1877, the notes were printed privately, but in 1877, the Bureau of Engraving and Printing—a division of the U.S. Department of the Treasury— assumed responsibility for printing all notes.

During the late nineteenth century, the U.S. government increased its reserve of precious metals by offering certificates in exchange for deposits of gold and silver. Into the first half of the twentieth century, the U.S. currency remained relatively stable, with Congress altering fixed exchange rates to gold and silver only occasionally.

In the late 1950s, rising world demand for silver as an industrial metal began pushing up its price. To avoid the possibility that the value of silver in coins might exceed the face value, the Treasury began selling silver from its stockpile in the open market to keep the price of silver low. However, demand continued to run high and soon threatened the Treasury's silver inventory, so Congress took steps to reduce the amount of silver in American coins. In 1964, the silver content of half dollars was reduced from 90 percent to 40 percent and, in 1970, was eliminated entirely. Silver also was eliminated from quarters and dimes in 1965. The elimination of silver from all U.S. coins completed the transition of American currency from money of intrinsic value to fiat money.

In 1971, the United States made a decision that marked the beginning of the end of the international system of fixed exchange rates—America closed its "gold window." Foreign central banks were thus prevented from converting their holdings of dollars into gold at the official price. For the first time in history, the world's principal currencies were shorn of all links to the value of any real commodity. Henceforth, the value of money—

that is, the stability of prices—was entirely at the discretion of governments. Before long, inflation was raging almost everywhere.

Governments throughout history have tampered with the link between currencies and underlying measures of value. Whenever wars or other emergencies required it, they have become monetary cheats—fiddling with the convertibility of their currencies and at times suspending it altogether, raising revenue either by depreciating their coins (explicitly reducing their weight) or debasing them (secretly reducing the proportion of precious metal).

Since ancient times, whenever private mints found that the fees (or seignorage) for weighing, certifying, and coining their customers' precious metal were earning them a nice profit, governments have monopolized the business for themselves. That way, they found, the currency could be more conveniently debased whenever their battles for territory demanded extra money. This technology of expropriation (monetary policy, as it is now known) took its greatest leap forward with the advent of fiat currency. Governments printed intrinsically worthless bits of paper, called them legal tender, and required their subjects on pain of imprisonment to give them goods and labor in exchange.

For governments, the idea was understandably attractive. They surrounded the process with the mystique of sovereignty to make the confidence trick more plausible. In many countries, counterfeiting was not merely considered fraud but treason. Similarly, in the present debate over European monetary union, it is said that the creation of a European central bank would be an attack on the sovereignty of the member states. Viewed in historical perspective, that warrants a hollow laugh: the sovereignty in question is the right of a government to steal from its citizens.

The only check on these otherwise excellent opportunities for theft was the promise to redeem paper money for an asset of intrinsic value, such as gold. For a long time that was a serious inconvenience, because until around the middle of this century people thought the promise ought to be kept. By 1971 it had already been badly undermined. The closing of the gold window finished the job. The power of the state took another large and possibly irreversible step forward.

The world will not return to the gold standard. As history has shown, modern governments are now big enough to rig the gold market or the market for any other single commodity without much trouble. The dropping of the gold standard by governments means that they have now lost interest in manipulating the price of gold, since it no longer has a relation to their currencies. This is important to investors in gold, which now takes on a private significance as a hedge of value.

The history of money has been given here at length for a very important reason. It is important to not only be aware that something is wrong and that United States currency and investments are at risk, but to understand fully the reasons why this is so. It is very important to realize that these patterns of history repeat constantly and have done so for centuries. The current political rhetoric of a new administration in Washington *cannot* change the inevitable course of history, nor can it reverse the downhill slide that is well under way.

All governments and fiat monies have their problems, but some are better than others, and looking at the comparative strengths and values is important to preserving your wealth.

The Swiss franc is more than a paper currency—it is the only currency in the world that still is backed by gold. Swiss law requires a minimum 40 percent gold reserve for the Swiss franc, and the actual reserves are about 56 percent. But this is misleading, because the gold is carried on the Swiss central bank's books at the old "official" purchase price of US$42 per ounce. So with the current prices of gold, the gold backing per Swiss franc is actually many, many times its face value. No other currency in the world is in this position.

Too often in the history of mankind, paper currencies have become worthless. The huge gold reserves behind the Swiss currency simply prove that Switzerland trusts gold more as a monetary reserve than foreign paper currencies. Today, gold is out in most of the world, the laughingstock of the marketplace. Paper money is king, but then, junk bonds were king in the 1980s.

The past 10-year record for gold has not been good, especially for those who simply chose it out of loyalty to the principle that gold and sound money are important. So is gold extinct? This chapter has clearly shown that it is not—paper money will fail again and again and again. There is no reliable way to know when, but we can accept the lesson of history that it will. The popularity of an investment has nothing to do with its soundness.

To protect wealth properly, an investor must act on his own, know why he is doing so, and not drift along waiting for a political solution that history has shown is impossible.

Though all paper currencies, including the Swiss, have their flaws, the Swiss currency is the strongest available today, as you will learn in the discussion of the Swiss franc and its gold backing. This provides it with stability that make Swiss investments an economically viable means of protecting wealth.

CHAPTER 2

A BRIEFER HISTORY OF U.S. DEBT

The United States has a history of debt that is unique. Understanding the psychology of this debt is important to the modern investor. Failing to understand it can be fatal, as happened during the 1980s junk bond fad when the American investment markets appeared to lose all perspective on the matter of debt. This and the savings and loan industry crisis/collapse were symptoms of a psychology of any level of debt being acceptable. For an investor this is dangerous thinking, and it can be difficult for a European investment professional looking at the United States to understand how Americans can get so carried away with insecure investments.

There have, of course, been fad investments in

Europe in earlier centuries, the tulip craze and the South Sea Bubble being two of the more famous ones. But the attitude of European investment professionals in recent decades is very conservative and does not embrace the speculative gambling that has become prevalent in the American financial markets.

Many of the original settlers before the American Revolution had financed their purchases of tools and land by debt. For a poor man to acquire debt in Europe was difficult, usually impossible; no one would lend him money, as he had no collateral. In America it was easy because he had the security of his labor and, above all, a limitless future. Land purchase by debt, speculation on credit, was thus written into the economic soul of the new nation. It was inevitable, it was fully justified by the speed at which the land was settled, and it was debt that was, in most cases, paid. But acquiring debt—borrowing against the future—became a national characteristic: indebtedness was not only not shameful, it was almost, in a sense, patriotic. Once independence was gained, financial institutions—above all, a plethora of banks—sprang up to serve this marked American propensity.

The U.S. government abetted the process. In 1800, for instance, it sold the public 320-acre farms but required only a quarter of the purchase price down. The rest was paid out of harvest profits over four years. Much of early land legislation provided for credit—the Desert Land Act of 1877, for instance, offered farms in huge areas of the west for as little as 25 cents an acre down, provided only that the purchaser promised to irrigate.

Congress also encouraged company debt by, for instance, providing land free to railroads that could borrow enough money from the banks to lay down track. America's ninteenth-century pursuit of her "manifest destiny," both in land settlement and in the communications revolution that made it possible, was essentially launched on credit.

Pursuing the ideal of independence in the 1770s, the founding fathers not only created the national debt but led the new nation into the worst inflation of its history. By 1780, the $240 million of paper continentals it had issued were almost worthless. In 1791, the national debt stood at 40 percent of gross national product (GNP). In 1835, President Andrew Jackson reduced the debt to virtually zero. *This satisfactory state of affairs has never been achieved by any other power, before or since.*

Thereafter, the debt increased in accordance with "national emergencies." By the end of the Civil War it had risen to more than $2.76 billion. By the end of the First World War it had climbed to $25 billion but was then prudently reduced by about a third during the prosperous 1920s. As a result of the Great Depression, it rose once more, standing at $48 billion in 1939. With World War II it soared still further, this time astronomically, to $271 billion by 1946. But again, the dictates of prudence began to operate. Between 1946, its high point, and 1975, the national debt was reduced by more than half.

That was satisfactory, conforming to the pattern of 200 years of sound federal fiscal policy. But then, in the late 1970s, a curious thing happened. Without an emergency, without a world war, without even the excuse of a severe recession, the national debt began to rise again, first slowly, then more rapidly. Since then it has reached a historic high.

That meant a growing proportion of government revenues were devoted, year by year, simply to servicing the debt, and in turn (since its expenditures were not substantially reduced), that meant added pressure to either raise taxes or expand the deficit and so increase the debt still further.

High-spending congressmen, pursuing aims that by their nature are ultimately unrealizable, have proved popular with voters locally. At the same time, the electorate as a whole, voting nationally, expressed its concern with the country's drift into financial profligacy by sending to the White House Republican candidates pledged to do something about it. In practice, this led to a terrible contradiction: Democratic congresses unwilling to cut domestic spending and Republican administrations unwilling to raise taxes. Thus the federal government came under the conflicting control of both extremists and moderates, of utopians and pragmatists, both blaming the other for what is, at bottom, a profoundly immoral procedure—spending money by borrowing against the future. The result is the deficit and the mounting debt.

Today, this public debt comes on top of a huge volume of private debt, which itself is increasing. The United States was created by the judicious use of private credit, but this was balanced by a strict regimen of public probity. Now the country has moved far away from the traditional American doctrine of individual financial responsibility. A consensus emerged that it was government's job to provide health care for everyone, food for those who didn't work, and secure retirements for those who had not saved. An enormous burden has been shifted onto the shoulders of future generations. The wrong has not been righted, and the folly continues. Whether the sea change in the 1994 Congressional election will really affect the trend of decades remains to be seen—and it may be many years before we can really tell.

A generation of economists, Washington policy experts, and publicists have argued that deficits are either desirable or irrelevant. Those arguments have often carried the day because opposing arguments have been so unsophisticated.

Foreign lenders might be able to help with the deficit, but if their debts continue to rise, foreigners are going to become more reluctant to hold dollars, and the status of the dollar as an international currency could go the way of the British pound sterling, once a major reserve currency and now virtually unwanted. The United States could suddenly find itself a second-class citizen in the world economy, subject to the same strictures as Nigeria.

As long as the dollar is the accepted international currency, America's foreign debt does not pose a serious problem. In fact, because the debt is in dollars, when the dollar declines internationally, the U.S. debt itself declines. But by continuing to run budget and trade deficits and to rely on foreign capital to buy U.S. Treasury bonds and stimulate private investment, the United States could eventually incite a revolt against the dollar. Paying debts in a country's own currency is such a tempting privilege that it always ends up being abused. The issuer of a widely accepted currency starts to consume more than it produces, and eventually the holders of its IOUs begin asking for a different kind of payment. This will eventually occur if the United States continues along its present deficit path—most likely by early in the next century, and that is only a decade away. For a long-term investor or one building a retirement fund, a decade is relatively short.

The are many political arguments as to what to do about the debt. They could continue for years. If an investor enjoys political debate, he can always join in the fray. But if the real concern is protecting his wealth and those who matter, he must rely on personal initiative, not a political solution. And if he really wants to participate in active politics, isn't it better to do so from a secure and protected position?

CHAPTER 3

INVESTING ABROAD IS NEITHER IMMORAL NOR UNPATRIOTIC

First, it is imperative that we establish the exact purposes for which financial havens are created and their political implications. This book examines a highly effective method of asset protection and growth. But who *really* wants to protect his assets and reduce his taxes? The question may seem stupidly naive. Who *doesn't* want to keep more of what's his? But this sort of answer, derived from the cynical "everyone is selfish" notion, is not what we are looking for.

Asset protection through the use of international financial strategies requires considerable initiative, alertness, determination, and dedication. Not that it doesn't pay. Sad to say, the net gain from each hour dedicated to protecting your wealth is almost certain to be higher than the net gain from an hour of productive employment. Thanks to "progressive" taxation, this goes double for someone in a relatively high tax bracket. There is also a psychological dimension that must not be neglected. Most people derive a "clean" feeling from making a living through their work but feel that there is something "dirty" about "scheming" to reduce their taxes.

Heavy taxes, whether used to provide luxury for a ruling elite or to support welfare schemes, always penalize individual initiative and productivity, decrease investment capital and thus the resources required for economic growth, reduce the standard of living, and force individuals to hide things, both activities and incomes, from the government and from one another. Heavy taxation, therefore, endangers the future of high-tax countries.

Internationalizing assets assumes at the outset that the investor has assets that are available for investment. It also assumes that a viable means of doing so exists in the contemporary scheme of world business, and ideally, a plan exists that includes short- and long-range investment goals.

To consider the question of the morality of tax avoidance, it is first necessary to set forth a working definition of morality. In the context of taxation, morality is not considered an absolute but a concept that, like the tax laws themselves, is subject to interpretation. One person might argue quite convincingly that it is morally wrong to tax a working widow with children to help provide the day-to-day support for a war veteran who is able to work but prefers not to, and still another person can argue just as convincingly on behalf of the veteran. Others would argue the libertarian position that all taxation is theft.

The morality of taxation changes with the times. Prior to World War I, when taxes were comparatively low, though certainly not popular, most workers and small businessmen were exempt from the controversy by virtue

of low incomes. During times of national emergency, particularly during and directly following World War II, tax
avoidance was frowned upon even by those who were
looking at larger tax liabilities each year. But as progressive tax rates drove taxes higher and higher each year in
highly industrialized and populated nations, the attitudes
of taxpayers underwent a gradual but definitive change.

Today, even the individual worker for whom the tax
system is supposedly designed can see that a system in
which higher income brackets produce progressively
higher tax rates is stultifying to individual initiative and
productivity. Therefore, investors feel not only duty-
bound but morally obligated to use the legal tax-avoid-
ance measures available to them. Whether the tax loss to
the nation is through the use of domestic tax shelter
strategies or an international financial center, the avoidance principle is exactly the same. From a purely prag-
matic viewpoint, legal tax avoidance by an investor may
not be the road to wealth but simply a means of economic
survival for himself and his family.

The "losers" in this business of tax avoidance are
presumed to be the heavily industrialized, heavily populated, and heavily taxed countries of the world. If two
nations could personify this description, they would be
the United States and Great Britain. Yet the attitudes of
these governments toward tax avoidance is ambivalent to
say the least. The United States, for example, actually
established itself as a tax haven for foreigners by not
imposing a withholding tax on interest paid to foreigners
on their U.S. bank deposits and allowing foreigners to
buy, hold, and sell U.S. securities without incurring a
capital gains liability.

There are, of course, economic reasons to justify
these tax rulings (a reversal of the ruling on interest paid
on bank deposits would remove billions of dollars from
U.S. banks). This being the case, we can say that there is
no external threat to tax avoidance from free world

nations. The United States and Switzerland are both involved in the business of providing a haven for foreign investors to protect their assets. The citizens of each frequently use the other for international diversification, and neither is likely to try to put the other out of business.

The bottom line is that the individual investor must protect his own assets. But how? The rest of this book will show that there is a way—a very elegant solution that is completely legal, completely secret, and risk-free.

CHAPTER 4

WHY SWITZERLAND?

Switzerland is situated geographically in the center of Europe, where major continental roads from east, west, north, and south intersect. Its internal roads and railways are excellent, and all Swiss transportation services are punctual. It is also accessible by river barge directly from the sea. Airline service is tops, and telecommunications are the very best available. Needless to say, professional services are of the very highest quality and reliability.

Furthermore, Switzerland has been successful at remaining neutral in many European conflicts and during both world wars, so in modern times its economy has never been devastated by war's destruction. Also, it is basically a free-enterprise country with minimal government regulation and economic control.

For these reasons, Switzerland has long served as a magnet for the money of wealthy foreigners who perceive the world as buffeted by overtaxation, overregulation, and political turmoil. They are attracted, too, of course, by the confidentiality and discretion that have been hallmarks of Swiss bankers since the French Revolution, when they offered financial refuge to French aristocrats.

Banking in Switzerland, a land of few natural resources, has been immensely lucrative. Operating in a country less than half the size of Maine, Swiss banks control more than $400 billion in assets, making the country the third largest financial center in the world.

For people with money to protect—whether a little or a lot—Switzerland is traditionally considered the world's safest repository. These days, the Swiss can give Americans many reasons to leave funds in Switzerland. But the promise of total secrecy in financial matters remains one of the greatest attractions of Swiss banks.

That promise isn't just a lot of hype. Secrecy and discretion in financial matters are anchored in the democratic principles of Switzerland. In 1934, the Swiss put teeth in their traditional code of bank secrecy by enacting the Swiss Banking Law. To stop Nazi agents from bribing Swiss bank employees for names of account holders, the law prescribed a hefty fine and prison sentence for any bank employee caught divulging information on bank customers. Moreover, the law decreed that bank employees must carry their secrets to the grave, not just until they leave the bank.

The Swiss Banking Law remains very much intact today, but instead of Nazi agents, the law now confounds agents of the U.S. Internal Revenue Service. If the account holder doesn't tell, the IRS cannot find out how much he has on deposit in a Swiss account or even that a Swiss account exists in his name, unless it can convince Swiss authorities that the person has committed a criminal offense *under Swiss law*. Those last three words are key, because many infractions that are considered criminal in the United States—most significantly, tax evasion—aren't criminal offenses in Switzerland.

Unhappy with their reputation as magnets for illicit dollars, many Swiss bankers downplay the secrecy shroud. Rather than secrecy, the best reason to open a Swiss account, they say, simply is to internationalize your investments. The argument goes like this: the risk in a portfolio is lessened when the assets are diversified among different investments. So why not diversify further by investing money in countries besides the United States? To do that, an investor needs access to international markets. Switzerland really is a financial supermarket in that regard.

SECRECY LAWS

Popular media stories have created two contradictory pictures of Swiss secrecy: that it hinders law enforcement officers from prosecuting criminals, or that it no longer exists and is as full of holes as Swiss cheese. Neither is true.

The basic position in Swiss civil law is that information concerning a customer and his financial dealings is protected as part of his legal right to privacy. In Switzerland, this has been made part of Article 28 of the Swiss Civil Code, and it not only protects the information but makes the person violating the secrecy liable for damages to the customer. In addition, the banking law makes it a criminal offense for a banker to divulge information about a customer in violation of the law, punishable by fine or imprisonment. Both the bank and the bank employee may be subject to various penalties if a violation occurs.

A bank can only disclose information when authorized to do so under existing statutory provisions or by a Swiss court order, which must be founded on law.

Secrecy is interpreted so broadly that it is illegal for a bank to say whether or not a person is a customer, since if the bank refused to do so it would be implying that the person was a customer.

The right of secrecy is a right belonging to the customer, not the bank. It is the customer's privacy that is protected by law. The customer can waive the secrecy, but the bank cannot. For example, the customer may waive secrecy and ask the bank to give a credit reference to a specific creditor. But such a waiver is only valid if the customer acts voluntarily and not under duress. Therefore, waivers that were signed pursuant to foreign court orders compelling a customer to sign a waiver may well be invalid. A financial institution cannot ask the government for an order waiving secrecy; only the customer can waive the secrecy.

Contrary to an opinion current in America, Swiss secrecy is not absolute. It can be overridden by statutory provisions that compel the giving of information. Such rules requiring disclosure of information—usually with a limited scope—can be found in Swiss inheritance law (one really wouldn't want the sole legitimate heir going into the insurance company with a death certificate only to be told it can't tell him anything), in enforcement of judgments from creditors, in bankruptcy, or in divorce.

The most widely known limitation on secrecy is in treaties concerning Swiss cooperation in foreign criminal matters. In a criminal investigation conducted in Switzerland of a Swiss crime committed by a Swiss citizen, secrecy can be lifted by court order. The treaties extend this possibility to foreign crimes by foreign citizens in foreign investigations, but only in the limited circumstances spelled out in the treaties.

Before a foreign legal assistance request for Swiss financial records can be honored, the following conditions must be met:

1. Compulsory disclosure is only possible if the offense that is being prosecuted is punishable as a *criminal offense* in both countries (the requesting state and Switzerland).

2. In tax cases, assistance is available to foreign prosecutors only if the investigated violation of foreign tax laws would be qualified under Swiss law as a tax fraud and not merely as tax evasion. Tax evasion is simply the failure to declare income or assets for taxation; tax fraud is distinguished by the fact that "fraudulent conduct" is involved. Normally, fraudulent conduct can only be assumed if forged documents are used.

   There is a special provision of the Swiss-United States Treaty on Mutual Assistance in Criminal Matters that provides Swiss legal assistance to U.S. prosecutors even in tax evasion cases *if they are conducting an investigation against an organized crime group.*

3. As a general rule, the information obtained in Switzerland through a legal assistance procedure may not be used for investigative purposes nor be introduced into evidence in the requesting state in any proceeding relating to an offense other than the offense for which assistance has been granted.

It must be emphasized that foreign authorities or foreign courts cannot directly ask a Swiss financial institution for information. Even in cases in which legal assistance can be granted and therefore secrecy is lifted, only a *Swiss* court order—which in these cases is based upon a foreign request for legal assistance—can validly lift secrecy.

Considering this, it can be said that secrecy is strict and is only put aside in cases clearly defined by Swiss law and pursuant to Swiss rules. Secrecy is, however, not absolute and therefore does not protect criminals.

NEUTRALITY

Americans have become somewhat complacent about the possibility of their funds being held hostage by world events, since it hasn't happened to American funds in major countries for a long time. In recent decades, it has been more often a case of the United States holding foreign funds hostage, including those of Haiti, Iran, and Kuwait. (During the Gulf War, Kuwaiti citizens could not access their funds, even though they were refugees who had fled Kuwait.)

The principle of neutrality protects all wealth equally. This principle of neutrality is important to understanding why the Swiss excel at the preservation of individual wealth. Your wealth simply cannot, and will not, be held hostage in Switzerland. By staying out of international conflicts and maintaining strict neutrality, Switzerland has become a refuge for capital from all over the world.

CHAPTER 5

SWITZERLAND AND EUROPE

Switzerland turned 700 years old in 1991, but there was no grand, flag-waving celebration. Throughout the year, cities and villages celebrated in their own way, with alpine yodeling and wrestling fests, fireworks over Lake Zurich, and ballet in Lausanne.

This country—made up of 26 highly independent cantons, embracing four languages—is simply too diverse to host a big, nationalistic bash such as the United States put on in 1976, the Swiss explain.

Seven hundred years ago, if legend is to be believed, three brawny peasants met on a pretty meadow called the Rutli at the foot of the steep climb to the St. Gotthard Pass, then, as now, the most direct route from the upper

Rhine to Venice and the silk routes leading east. The perpetual alliance they swore is usually considered the nucleus of the Swiss Confederation.

The three men in that meadow 700 years ago were tribal chieftains of what later became the cantons of Schwyz, Uri, and Unterwalden. They signed a treaty for mutual protection in the crisis of succession after the death of the Habsburg ruler Rudolf I. The Habsburgs' ancestral castle was not far away, and the men of the forest cantons worried that some more remote king might be less amenable to leaving them alone to collect bridge-tolls and provide guided mule trains.

Twenty years later, the neighbors in Lucerne were invited to join the loose confederation. Its influence spread, sometimes by persuasion and often by conquest, but only after a resounding defeat at the hands of the French at Marignano in Lombardy in 1515 did the mountaineers decide to eschew foreign military adventures. That kept them from neither fighting among themselves for a few centuries more nor, since the country was desperately poor in natural resources, from hiring themselves out as mercenaries for others (the last survivors of that practice are the Vatican's Swiss Guards). Unlike the rest of Europe, Swiss history remained stable through the ensuing centuries, with no invasions or major changes in the political structure.

In December 1992, the Swiss electorate voted against affiliation with the European Community (now the European Union, or EU). What should we make of the Swiss vote? Here is the richest country in Europe (and by some measures the richest in the world), in the middle of the world's largest trading bloc, saying that it can stand back from closer union. On the face of it, it looks as though the Swiss have made a serious and uncharacteristic error, at least in economic terms. Though the vote will not lead to any economic catastrophe, conventional wisdom suggests that it will inhibit future growth. Swiss firms live by their exports, and, to some extent at least, they will find it harder to export across the border. They may be forced to push some production over to subsidiaries within the EU. Perhaps some investment that would have gone to Switzerland will go elsewhere.

It was fear that the brilliant Swiss economy would be so damaged that encouraged the political leaders to press for membership in the EU. Is this a case of ordinary voters allowing their hearts to rule their heads against the advice of the establishment?

The conventional view was that the decision would hinder future economic growth. It reckoned that as far as the stock market was concerned, a combination of higher trade costs and lower gross domestic product growth would more than offset any advantages from nonmembership, such as lower interest rates and freedom from EU competition policy. By this theory, the economic effects of a "no" vote would justify a permanent fall in Swiss share prices.

This was an intriguing exercise, but of course a move in the stock market of between 5 and 10 percent is not that much, given the scale of the swings that take place in securities prices every week. The implication for growth is perhaps more worrisome. A major investment banking firm, Goldman Sachs, immediately published a crisis report reckoning that the diversion of investment following the "no" vote along with labor migration (skilled people leaving) might together chip 0.6 percent off annual growth over 10 years. That would be quite a lot, if it were to happen.

But will it? There is a counterargument to be made, which is that staying outside the EU might actually enhance Switzerland's economic performance. It runs like this.

Switzerland happens to be in an extremely strong structural position. It has great strength in industries that look like winners for the next decade or more. These include financial services (the three big banks—Swiss Bank Corporation, Credit Swisse, Union Bank of Switzerland—and the Geneva-based fund management industry), pharmaceuticals (the three big chemical companies—CIBA-GEIGY A.G., Roche Holding A.G., Sandoz Ltd.), food (Nestle, Suchard), and up-market tourism (St. Moritz, Klosters, and Verbier). These are all areas of the world economy in which Japan and the newly industrialized countries cannot compete actively, and where the price of the product is not being shaved constantly by some new technological advance. By contrast, Switzerland is not strong in cars, aircraft, electronic consumer durables, and computers—all areas where European industry is, or is about to be, threatened by the Far East.

In that sense it is better protected than most of the countries in the EU. Switzerland does have important industries in areas such as machine tools, which are more open to international competition and might suffer if the economy was distanced from the rest of Europe, but much of its strength is in areas where it is quite well protected.

Indeed, in some of these areas being outside the EU is an advantage. Take financial services, which accounts for 30 percent of the value of the securities on the Swiss stock market. Swiss banks trade on their security and their discretion. It was fascinating to see that foreign money actually flowed *into* Swiss securities following the vote. Switzerland was perceived as a safer place to put cash if it remained outside the EU, presumably because of fear that at some future date the EU bureaucrats would get their fingers on those numbered bank accounts.

In most of the other areas noted above, EU membership is not really an issue. In pharmaceuticals there might be some modest disadvantage to staying outside, but the market is such an international "brain-based" one that it is hard to see any serious damage. Food products? Well, Nestle generates roughly 97 percent of its sales outside Switzerland but is not really dependent on exports across the Swiss national boundary into the rest of Europe. Tourism? Membership in the EU is not an issue.

So while there might be some modest disadvantage to Switzerland, the traditionally strong Swiss industries would be fine. Some sectors, in particular financial services, would do better by staying outside. The effect might therefore be merely to push the country even further toward its specialties. But since these are good growth areas, one could argue that Switzerland will benefit by remaining apart from the rest of Europe.

CHAPTER 6

THE SWISS FRANC:

Pillar of Financial Stability

As discussed in Chapter 1, the Swiss franc is backed by gold, and the actual gold reserves amount to many times the amount of Swiss francs in circulation. No other currency in the world is in this position.

Switzerland's political and economic stability has contributed to the Swiss franc's superior level of performance. The Swiss franc has steadily increased in value against all other currencies. Long term, the Swiss franc has been the world's best investment currency.

There is no question that the Swiss franc has been the best managed currency in the world. Others have been rising stars—the German mark and the Japanese yen, for example—but they rose as a result of speculation on the rapid growth of their underlying economies, not because the currency was well managed. And they didn't remain stars. The yen has been affected by severe Japanese economic problems and the mark by the high cost of reunification of Germany, a cost that may go on for decades yet.

Historically, the Japanese yen has been a heavy loser of monetary value against the Swiss franc. The Japanese paper and debt crisis may turn out to be worse than the American one.

The German cost of reunification has already vastly exceeded the politicians' estimates. Taxes and deficit spending are skyrocketing. The reasons are understandable, but understanding doesn't change the economic effect on the mark, which may become a far weaker currency than many economists predict.

For many, Swiss interest rates seem low, yet viewed historically, the long-term return has run higher than 10 percent when measured in U.S. dollars. Many investors make the mistake of comparing yields expressed only in the currency of the investment and fail to calculate the relative yields, including the currency fluctuations.

In the end, the historical strength of the Swiss franc against the dollar stems primarily from the Swiss people's demonstrated desire and ability to follow relatively sound policies and to deviate from these only reluctantly and temporarily. In contrast, U.S. and other foreign policy makers have shown a growing appetite for policies that promote inflation. Until we see evidence that these fundamentally different approaches will change, we can expect the Swiss franc to appreciate further in the long run, although this trend may continue to be interrupted by short-term reversals.

CHAPTER 7

HOW TO OPEN A TAX-FREE SWISS MONEY MARKET ACCOUNT

A brand new product, BankSwiss, is an attractive alternative to the conventional Swiss savings account. Interest rates are higher, and earnings are free of the 35 percent withholding tax imposed by Switzerland on bank account interest received by foreigners. Earnings accumulate tax free since, technically, your capital is pooled into liquidity funds (money market funds). Being linked directly to short-term money market rates, higher yields can be achieved. You can add funds to BankSwiss at your discretion, make withdrawals when required, even issue payment instructions without any restrictions. So for the investor wishing to establish a Swiss bank base as a precaution for the future or a springboard for other international investments, BankSwiss is the lucrative choice.

The minimum to open a BankSwiss account is US$10,000 or the equivalent in another currency. With a BankSwiss account of $50,000 or more (or equivalent in another currency), you may obtain an international credit card. You always have easy access to your funds for purchases or cash withdrawals via ATM (automatic teller machine). Any payments or withdrawals are simply charged to your BankSwiss account.

Traditionally, Switzerland has a global orientation, so it comes as no surprise that you can find the world's most flexible and internationally oriented investments in this country. BankSwiss is no exception. To accommodate the growing number of international clients, BankSwiss is available in four major currencies: Swiss francs (SFr), deutsche marks (DM), U.S. dollars (US$), and European currency unit (ECU). You can open your BankSwiss in one or several of these currencies at your discretion, and, in addition, you can switch the denomination of your BankSwiss at any time, investing in the currency you deem most favorable. (Whichever currency you choose, remember, higher interest rates are always accompanied by higher risk. Taking all factors into consideration, it is hard to beat the traditional strength and security of the Swiss franc.)

(If you are not familiar with the ECU, it was created in 1979. It is composed of a currency basket of 11 European currencies, and its value is calculated daily by the European Commission according to the changes in value of the underlying currencies. The ECU is composed of a weighted average of all member currencies of the European Monetary System. Since the ECU changes its balance to reflect changes in exchange rates and interest rates between these currencies, it tends to limit exchange rate and interest rate risks.)

Diversifying assets across a spectrum of different types of investments is a well-known and long-practiced strategy. Today, private investors around the world are increasingly demanding international diversification to preserve wealth, optimize gains, and minimize risk. BankSwiss can serve as a springboard for global investment opportunities and is an excellent place to start or broaden your international investment strategy.

With BankSwiss you can switch your investment into global funds or, going a step further, you can invest your capital in any other specific investment you choose. For example, should the time be right for stocks, you can purchase them with BankSwiss. Should you be interested in precious metals, you can invest in them as well. Should you sell your stocks or precious metals, BankSwiss serves as a "parking lot"—storing liquidity safely and profitably for possible future investment opportunities. Your funds won't lie stagnant but will continue to earn interest yet remain immediately available to you at all times. BankSwiss is an investment vehicle with almost boundless investment opportunities—a single account for all seasons.

BankSwiss is a product of UeberseeBank, a mid-sized Swiss investment bank in the heart of Zurich's banking district. Established in 1965, UeberseeBank specializes in securities accounts management and investment counseling for an international clientele, with more than 14,000 clients and assets exceeding 4 billion Swiss francs under management. Renowned for its innovative investment accounts for foreign investors, UeberseeBank takes pride in its exemplary customer service.

UeberseeBank is a 100 percent subsidiary of the American International Group (AIG), a AAA-rated international insurance group with headquarters in New York. AIG has over 35,000 employees in more than 130 countries worldwide.

For more information on BankSwiss, write to:

JML Jurg M. Lattmann AG
Swiss Investment Counsellors
Baarerstrasse 53, Dept. 212
CH-6304 Zug, Switzerland

JML will submit your application to UeberseeBank and supervise the opening of your account. Upon receipt of your completed application form and deposit, UeberseeBank will confirm the opening of your BankSwiss account in writing.

CHAPTER 8

THE SWISS INSURANCE INDUSTRY

Insurance companies belong to one of the most important sectors of the economy in Switzerland. They are also extremely conservative and safe. In 130 years, none have failed, a record that even Swiss banks cannot match. Unique tax advantages combined with conservative money management allow Swiss insurance products to perform much better than one might expect. And conservative does not have to mean low returns. If an insurance company doesn't have to deduct losses on a lot of bad investments, it is much easier to maintain a conservative, safe, high return.

Swiss insurance regulation keeps investment portfolios at a nearly no-risk level. Liquidity and valuation of investments are ultraconservative. For example, a maximum of only 30 percent of investible funds may be put in real estate. Swiss real estate has always held the highest values, but this is ultraconservatism at work—if it should go down, it might not be liquid enough to cover claims, so be ultraconservative and severely limit the exposure. It is a philosophy that a lot of American banks and insurance companies are probably now wishing they had followed— or at least their policyholders are wishing they had.

Just in case this isn't enough, Swiss insurance companies often carry their real estate holdings at less than half their present market value, allowing a very wide margin of price changes before safety can possibly be affected.

Swiss accounting in general seems to be on the conservative side. Companies tend to have hidden reserves of millions rather than the North American style of overvaluing assets to achieve a high stock market price for takeover bids. This conservatism applies all the more to the insurance industry.

Swiss insurance companies offer a greater range of services than the American investor is used to. In fact, the range is broader than that offered by most Swiss banks. There are only about 20 insurance companies in Switzerland. This concentration makes the industry not only stronger but easier to supervise than its U.S. counterpart, which has thousands of insurance companies. There are no weak insurance companies in Switzerland, unlike in the United States where laws in many states permit an insurance company to be formed with capital as low as $100,000, and licensed, empty insurance company shells are frequently sold in classified ads in the *Wall Street Journal* and other newspapers.

In Switzerland, the industry is overseen by the Swiss Federal Bureau of Private Insurance, a very strict regulator. There is no rate competition; the emphasis is on maintaining the strength of the insurer and prohibiting risky investments (although it is unlikely that a

Swiss insurance manager would even *think* of making a risky investment).

Regulation of private insurance companies has been governed by a clause in the Swiss federal constitution since 1885. Contrast this to the United States, where insurance companies are often regulated only by rules promulgated by a politically appointed insurance commissioner, who expects to be employed by an insurance company when the governor who appointed him leaves office in a few years.

WHAT IS AN ANNUITY?

An annuity is money invested with an insurance company that provides a tax-advantaged way to put aside money for retirement or other objectives. Annuities may be among the best ways to create retirement income. They allow savings to grow tax-deferred, building assets faster than other investments. And because an annuity is also an insurance product, it promises a guaranteed regular income after retirement regardless of how long the investor lives.

Annuities may be a good investment for many long-term goals, but several features make them especially well-suited for retirement savings:

- *No annual investment ceiling.* There is no limit to the amount that can be put into an annuity each year. Other tax-advantaged plans such as IRAs (individual retirement accounts) should not be overlooked for retirement savings, but the amount that can be contributed each year is limited.
- *The power of tax-deferral.* For several reasons, money will grow faster than in a taxable vehicle with a similar rate of return. Not only does the interest accumulate tax-free until withdrawal, but funds that otherwise would have been used to pay taxes

remain in the account for additional earnings. And if the payments are not taken until retirement, the recipient will probably be in a lower tax bracket at that time.

- *Security for one's family.* If the purchaser dies before distributions begin, his family (or other beneficiaries) can receive the full value of the annuity. By naming a beneficiary, the annuity may even bypass probate and eliminate the associated costs and publicity.
- *Simplicity.* There are no annual IRS forms to file, and there is no entry on Form 1040 until the payments actually begin.

Though unglamorous, an annuity is one of the investment industry's fastest-growing products. Although it has been available for more than 20 years, sales have boomed in the last few years—sales of domestic annuities in the United States are now running around $50 billion per year. But the real reason for the growth is that as the American population ages, it is waking up to the fact that retirement self-sufficiency is an important issue. The annuity has some ideal characteristics for them.

An annuity, often described as the opposite of life insurance, is a financial contract with an insurance company. It can be structured so the insurance company makes regular monthly payments for life, no matter how long the recipient lives.

Although technically the investor doesn't own the investments the annuity makes—the insurance company does—he still benefits from their investment. Just as with an IRA, no taxes are due on investment gains while the funds remain in the annuity account. This helps savings grow faster, and it allows individuals to better control when they will pay taxes. But taxes are due when money is withdrawn, and just as with an IRA or a 401(k) account, withdrawal of funds before age 59 1/2 incurs a 10 percent penalty.

Although these investments do enjoy tax-deferred status like other retirement accounts, individuals still get greater tax savings under traditional IRA or 401(k) plans. But once beyond the level of what can be deducted, annuities are for investors who want to build substantial tax-free growth and not be limited to a government-mandated maximum amount of savings.

In an IRA or other retirement account, initial investments under certain limits are deposited before taxes. This allows wage earners to shield current income from tax as well as allow investments to accumulate on a tax-deferred basis. With an annuity, the initial investment is made with post-tax dollars, although after that, investment gains are tax-free until withdrawn.

So an annuity should be considered a supplemental retirement tool. Other tax-advantaged plans such as IRAs should not be overlooked for retirement savings, but the amount that can be contributed each year is limited. In an annuity one can set aside as much money each year as retirement or other future plans require.

Owning an annuity also can prevent some tax liability that often hits mutual fund holders. When a mutual fund is purchased, a capital gains distribution is paid at the end of the year, and even if the mutual fund holder reinvests it, it is a taxable event. With a variable annuity, any profit made, as long as it stays there, grows tax-deferred.

Because annuities are insurance products, the fees paid by investors are different than for mutual funds. Typically, there are no front-end load fees or commissions to buy an annuity, but there are "surrender" charges for investors who withdraw funds early in an American annuity, usually during the first five or six years. (This is not the case in the Swiss annuities discussed later.)

For several reasons, the money in an annuity will grow much faster than in a taxable vehicle with a similar rate of return. Not only does interest accumulate tax-free until withdrawal, but funds that would otherwise have been used to pay taxes remain in the account for additional earnings. And by the time of retirement, the recipient is usually in a lower tax bracket and will thus pay less tax on the annuity payments.

Although salesmen like to point out that an annuity's value is "guaranteed," that promise is only as strong as the insurer making it. An annuity is backed by the insurer's investment portfolio, which in America may contain junk bonds and troubled real estate investments. If an American insurer has financial problems, the investor may become just another creditor hoping to be paid back. For example, when the New Jersey state insurance department took over bankrupt Mutual Benefit Life, the state temporarily froze the accounts of annuity holders, preventing them from withdrawing money unless they could prove a significant financial hardship.

Some American annuity marketers inflate their yields by playing games with the way they calculate them. Others advertise sumptuous rates that have more strings attached than a marionette. The most widespread form of rate deception is the bonus annuity, in which insurers tack on as much as eight percentage points to their current interest rate. But many of these alluring bonuses can be illusory. In most cases, the bonus rate is only paid if the annuity is held for many years and then taken out in monthly installments instead of a lump sum. If the investor asks for the cash in a lump sum, the insurer will retroactively subtract the bonus, plus the interest that compounded on the bonus, plus a penalty on the original investment.

Even more insidious are tiered-rate annuities, so named because they have two levels of interest rates. They ballyhoo an above-average interest rate, but, as with their bonus-rate cousins, the accrued earnings in the account reflect this so-called accumulation rate only when the payout is made over a long time. A straight withdrawal, by contrast, will knock the annuity down to a low "surrender value" rate for every year invested.

Other insurers simply resort to the time-dishonored practice of luring customers with lofty initial rates that are lowered at renewal time.

All of this nonsense has given the American annuity industry a bad name, and it is not surprising that most investors simply hang up the telephone when an annuity salesman calls.

Enter the clean, simple, honest Swiss annuity.

SWISS ANNUITIES

Swiss annuities minimize the risk posed by U.S. annuities. They are heavily regulated, unlike in the United States, to avoid any potential funding problem. They denominate accounts in the strong Swiss franc compared to the weakening U.S. dollar. And the annuity payout is guaranteed.

Swiss annuities are also exempt from the famous 35 percent withholding tax imposed by Switzerland on bank account interest received by foreigners. Annuities do not have to be reported to Swiss or U.S. tax authorities.

A U.S. purchaser of an annuity is required to pay a 1 percent U.S. federal excise tax on the purchase of any policy from a foreign company. This is much like the sales tax rule that says that if a person shops in a state with a lower sales tax than his home state, when he gets home he is required to mail a check to his home state's sales tax department for the difference in sales tax rates.

The U.S. federal excise tax form (IRS Form 720) does not ask for details of the policy bought or who it was bought from. It merely asks for a calculation of 1 percent tax of any foreign policies purchased. This is a one-time tax at the time of purchase; it is not an ongoing tax. It is the responsibility of the U.S. taxpayer to report the Swiss annuity or other foreign insurance policy. *Swiss insurance companies do not report anything to any government agency, Swiss or American—not the initial pur-*

chase of the policy, the payments into it, or interest and dividends earned.

SPECIAL ADVANTAGES OF SWISS ANNUITIES

- *They pay competitive dividends and interest.*
- *No foreign reporting requirements.* A Swiss franc annuity is not a "foreign bank account" subject to the reporting requirements on the IRS Form 1040 or the special U.S. Treasury form for reporting foreign accounts. Transfers of funds by *personal* check or wire are not reportable under U.S. law by individuals. The reporting requirements apply *only* to cash and "cash equivalents" such as money orders, cashier's checks, and travelers' checks.
- *No forced repatriation of funds.* If America were to eventually institute exchange controls, the government might require that most overseas investments be repatriated to America. This has been a common requirement by most governments that have imposed exchange controls. Insurance policies, however, would likely escape any forced repatriation under future exchange controls because they are a pending contract between the investor and the insurance company. Swiss bank accounts would probably not escape such controls. (To the bureaucrats writing such regulations, an insurance policy is considered a commodity already bought rather than an investment.)
- *Protection from creditors.* No creditor, including the IRS, may attach a Swiss annuity if the purchaser's wife or children are named as beneficiaries (or if anyone else is named as an irrevocable beneficiary). No lien can attach to the annuity, and the purchaser knows that at least a portion of his wealth is beyond the reach of a litigious society and will, indeed, go to his designated heirs.

- *Instant liquidity.* With the Swiss Plus plan (described later), an investor can liquidate up to 100 percent of the account without penalty (except for a SFr500 charge during the first year and loss of interest).
- *Swiss security.* As already noted, Switzerland has the world's strongest insurance industry, with no failures in 130 years.
- *No Swiss tax.* If an investor accumulates Swiss francs through standard investments, he will be subject to the 35 percent withholding tax on interest or dividends earned in Switzerland. Swiss franc annuities are free of this tax. In the United States, insurance proceeds are not taxed. And earnings on annuities during the deferral period are not taxable until income is paid or when they are liquidated.
- *Convenience.* Sending deposits to Switzerland is no more difficult than mailing an insurance premium in the United States. A personal check in U.S. dollars is written and sent overseas (60¢ postage instead of 32¢). Funds can also be transferred by bank wire.
- *Qualified for U.S. pension plans.* Swiss annuities can be placed in U.S. tax-sheltered pension plans, such as IRA, Keogh, or corporate plans, or such a plan can be rolled over into a Swiss annuity. (To put a Swiss annuity into a U.S. pension plan, all that is required is a U.S. trustee, such as a bank or other institution, to hold the annuity contract in the United States. Many banks offer "self-directed" pension plans for a very small annual administration fee, and these plans can easily be used for this purpose.)
- *No load fees.* Investment in Swiss annuities is on a "no load" basis, front-end or back-end. The investments can be canceled at any time without a loss of principal and with all principal, interest, and dividends payable if canceled after one year. (Again, if you cancel in the first year, there is a small penalty of about 500 Swiss francs, plus loss of interest.)

SWISS PLUS

First offered in 1991, Swiss Plus brings together the benefits of Swiss bank accounts and Swiss deferred annuities without the drawbacks, presenting the best Swiss investment advantages for American investors.

Swiss Plus is a convertible annuity account offered only by Elvia Life of Geneva. Elvia Life is a $2 billion-strong company, serving 220,000 clients, of which 57 percent live in Switzerland and 43 percent abroad. The account can be denominated in the Swiss franc, U.S. dollar, German mark, or ECU, and the investor can switch at any time from one to another. Or an investor can diversify the account by investing in more than one currency and still change the currency at any time during the accumulation period up until he begins to receive income or withdraw the capital.

Although called an annuity, Swiss Plus acts more like a savings account than a deferred annuity. However, it is operated under an insurance company's umbrella, so it conforms to the IRS' definition of an annuity and, as such, compounds tax-free until it is liquidated or converted into an income annuity later on.

Swiss Plus accounts earn approximately the same return as long-term government bonds in the same currency the account is denominated in (European Union bonds in the case of the ECU), less a half-percent management fee. Interest and dividend income are guaranteed by a Swiss insurance company, and Swiss government regulations protect investors against either underperformance or overcharging.

Swiss Plus offers instant liquidity, a rarity in non-Swiss annuities. All capital, plus all accumulated interest and dividends, is freely accessible after the first year. During the first year, 100 percent of the principal is freely accessible, less a SFr500 fee and loss of the interest. So if all funds are needed quickly, either for an emergency or for another investment, there is no "lock-in" period as there is with most American annuities.

Upon maturity of the account, the investor can choose to receive a lump sum payout (paying capital gains tax on accumulated earnings only), roll the funds into an income annuity (paying capital gains taxes only as future income payments are received, and then only on the portion representing accumulated earnings), or extend the scheduled term by giving notice in advance of the originally scheduled date (and continue to defer tax on accumulated earnings).

PROTECTION OF ASSETS IN SWISS ANNUITIES FROM LAWSUITS

Growing your wealth is important, but so is protecting it from false claimants, and Switzerland excels at this. Almost anybody with wealth in the United States is at risk. With everything that can happen to savings, it is nice to know that there is something, somewhere, that nobody can touch.

According to Swiss law, insurance policies—including annuity contracts—cannot be seized by creditors. They also cannot be included in a Swiss bankruptcy procedure. Even if an American court expressly orders the seizure of a Swiss annuity account or its inclusion in a bankruptcy estate, the account will not be seized by Swiss authorities, provided that it has been structured the right way.

There are two requirements. A U.S. resident who buys a life insurance policy from a Swiss insurance company must designate his or her spouse, descendants, or a third party (if done so irrevocably) as beneficiary. Also, to avoid suspicion of making a fraudulent conveyance to avoid a specific judgment, under Swiss law, the person must have purchased the policy or designated the beneficiaries not less than six months before any bankruptcy decree or collection process.

A revocable designation of spouse or children can be converted into an irrevocable designation when the policyholder becomes aware of the fact that his creditors will seize his assets and that a court might compel him to repatriate the funds in the insurance policy. Because the spouse and children are already beneficiaries, changing their designation from revocable to irrevocable is sanctioned by Swiss law and is not considered a transfer to avoid creditors. The policyholder may change this designation before the policy expires if at such time there is no threat from any creditors. If the beneficiary is somebody other than a spouse or children, then the designation must already have been made irrevocable to protect the policy, as the purpose of the Swiss law is to protect the family, not to help people avoid creditors.

Article 81 of the Swiss insurance law provides that if a policyholder has made a revocable designation of spouse or children as beneficiaries, they automatically become policyholders and acquire all rights if the policyholder is declared bankrupt. In such a case, the original policyholder automatically loses control over the policy and also his right to demand the liquidation of the policy and the repatriation of funds. A court, therefore, cannot compel the policyholder to liquidate the policy or otherwise repatriate his funds. If the spouse or children notify the insurance company of the bankruptcy, the insurance company will note that in its records. Even if the original policyholder sends instructions to liquidate the policy because a court has ordered him to do so, the insurance company will ignore those instructions. It is important that the company be notified promptly of the bankruptcy so that it does not inadvertently follow the original policyholder's instructions because it wasn't told of the bankruptcy.

These laws were not created to make Switzerland an asset-protection haven—they are part of fundamental Swiss law. There is a current fad among some offshore islands to pass special legislation that allows the creation of asset-protection trusts for foreigners. Since they are not part of the fundamental legal structure of the country concerned, local legislators really don't care if they work or not. And since most of these trusts are simply used as a convenient legal title to assets that are left in the United States, such as brokerage accounts, houses, or office buildings, it is very easy for an American court to simply call the trust a sham to defraud creditors and ignore its legal title—seizing the assets that are within the physical jurisdiction of the court.

Such flimsy structures, providing only a thin legal screen to the title to American property, are quite different from real assets solely under the control of a rock-solid insurance company in a major industrialized country. A defendant trying to convince an American court that his local brokerage account is really owned by a trust represented by a brass-plate under a palm tree on a far-away island is not likely to be successful. More likely the court will simply seize the asset.

But with the Swiss annuity, the insurance policy is not being protected by the Swiss courts and government because of any special concern for the American investor but because the principle of protection of insurance policies is a fundamental part of Swiss law for the protection of the Swiss themselves. Insurance is for the family, not something to be taken by creditors or other claimants. No Swiss lawyer would even waste his time bringing such a case.

SWISS INCOME ANNUITIES CAN BE TAILOR-MADE

The main purpose of an annuity is to provide you with a constant income for as long as you live. But people's needs and circumstances differ, and to accommodate them a variety of beneficiary options is available for both single and joint annuities.

In weighing the merits of the different annuity

plans, several factors come into play. Your gender, your age and that of your spouse when your life income begins, and the size of your deposit all have a bearing, as does the kind of beneficiary option you want.

Your age plays a crucial role in these considerations. The older you are, the more income difference there will be between an annuity without refund and one with any of the beneficiary options. If you can take out such an annuity at age 55, the difference in life income created under each option is not that much, because at age 55 the life expectancy for both males and females exceeds 25 years. According to statistics, therefore, the insurance company will probably have to pay out the entire amount regardless of what option the contract includes.

The older you are, however, the more relevant the option becomes. Whether the contract expires at death with no further payments (without refund) or some or all of the unused portion is refunded to a beneficiary (10 years certain, with refund—explained below), the life income will vary accordingly.

Choosing among the various beneficiary options requires that you ask yourself a few questions. For example, is there anyone whose well-being depends on your financial support? If there is indeed someone, such as a spouse, then you should consider a plan that provides for that person (or persons, if children are involved) after your death. In the case of a spouse, this might involve one of the following options: 10 years certain, with refund, a joint annuity, or perhaps a single annuity for your spouse as well as for you.

If you have no immediate dependant (or would leave no survivor who would be in hardship without you) and you are over 65, you may do best with a straight life annuity paying the highest income for as long as you live. This means that after your death the insurance company stops all payments. This option offers the highest life income per franc of premium deposit, regardless of whether you live one day or 30 years after the annuity is taken out. But the price you pay is that your beneficiaries get nothing.

To provide for beneficiaries, annuities are available "with refund," or for "10, 15 (or any number) years certain." Let's look at these options.

"With refund" simply means that at death, the unused portion of the premium paid is refunded to the beneficiary in a lump sum. The payment is determined by subtracting from the original premium the amount of guaranteed income paid out.

"Ten years certain" means the income is paid for a minimum of 10 years. In other words, should you die after receiving only two payments, your beneficiary will receive the income for eight more years. The principle is the same for a joint annuity; if the second person dies after only two annuity payments, the beneficiary will receive the remaining eight. Of course, in either case, the income is guaranteed for the life of the insured parties.

AN ADVANTAGEOUS "BANK ACCOUNT" WITH YOUR SWISS INSURANCE COMPANY

Most international investors finance Swiss annuities by single deposits. On the other hand, other investors choose to dollar-cost-average into these investments by making annual deposits, and many arrange for these payments through a Swiss bank account.

You don't have to have a Swiss bank account to pay your insurance premiums. In fact, such an account would be reportable under U.S. laws, thus removing one of the advantages of Swiss insurance. Instead, there is another way to make your premium payments—through a premium deposit account.

This method has so many advantages, it is surprising that so few people know about it. In effect, a premium deposit account is an interest-bearing "bank" account opened at your insurance company. It has two distinct advantages over a regular Swiss bank account.

First, it is not reportable to the tax authorities, because you are making payments to an insurance company, not a bank. Second, it pays interest rates about 1 percent higher than bank deposit (savings) accounts. Moreover, there is no withholding tax on the interest; all payments are tax-free.

On the other hand, you cannot buy gold, securities, or anything else with this account. It can only be an interest-bearing Swiss franc account designed to make automatic premium payments. When the annual premium is due, it is simply debited from your account.

You can predeposit as much as you want to your account (the minimum deposit is SFr100). Simply send the funds to your insurance company and use your policy number as you would your bank account number. By the way, as with a bank account, you'll receive an annual statement of your premium deposit account.

One final point: since insurance companies make surcharges of 2, 3, and 5 percent for semiannual, quarterly, and monthly premium payments respectively, you should simply stick with annual payments and use your premium deposit account for small deposits during the year, whenever you feel the exchange rate is particularly favorable or you simply have extra cash available.

U.S. TAX TREATMENT OF SWISS ANNUITIES

The estate tax implications of annuities will depend on which beneficiary option the contract includes. As far as taxes on the income payments are concerned, the calculations are based on the amount of life income received each year.

The lion's share of this income is tax free. Let's get a picture of how much is beyond the grasp of the taxman.

The IRS divides the total premium payment by the number of years theoretically left to you, based on life expectancy tables for your age at the time you start receiving payments.

Let's say a 65-year-old man, expected to live 15 years, purchases a $10,000 Swiss annuity. This premium payment divided by 15 years equals $666.67 per year. This is the nontaxable part.

Although the life income from this annuity is a fixed amount in Swiss francs, the dollar income he receives each year will fluctuate. Let's say he actually received $850 during the first year. Only the difference, $850 minus $666.67, or $183.33, is taxable as ordinary income. If he receives, say, $950 during the second year, he'll pay tax on $283.33. Thus, any profits resulting from currency appreciation are taxed as ordinary income in the year they are received. (Likewise, any currency depreciation can be claimed as a loss.)

If the annuitant lives beyond his life expectancy, all payments received after this period elapses are taxed as ordinary income. Referring to the foregoing example, if our 65-year-old annuitant, expected to live a further 15 years, actually dies at, say, age 85, the last five years of his life income will be taxed as ordinary income. On the other hand, should he die earlier than expected, the unrecovered portion of his premium is deductible on his final income tax return.

It is your responsibility to report earnings to your government. No Swiss company or office reports anything—not the purchase of a policy or the opening of an account, or payments, or currency profits. It is solely up to you.

The IRS recently ruled that a U.S. taxpayer can swap an annuity issued by a U.S. insurer for one issued by a foreign insurer that does not engage in business in the United States. The exchange is tax-free when all the requirements for Section 1035 are met. The IRS says that there is no requirement that both insurance contracts be issued by U.S. insurers for the exchange to be tax-free (Letter Ruling 9319024).

CHAPTER 9

USING A SWISS INVESTMENT CONSULTANT

The most practical way for North Americans to get information on Swiss annuities is to send a letter to a Swiss insurance broker specializing in foreign business. This is because very few transactions can be concluded directly by foreigners either with a Swiss insurance company or with regular Swiss insurance agents. Legally they can legally handle the business, but they aren't used to it.

JML Swiss Investment Counsellors is an independent group of financial advisors. Since 1974 this company has specialized in Swiss franc insurance, gold, and selected Swiss bank-managed investments for overseas and European clients. To date, the group is servicing more than 20,000 clients worldwide, with investments through

JML of more than 1 billion Swiss francs. Its services are free of charge to you because they are paid by the renowned companies with which you invest your money. Its commissions and fees are standard, and all transactions are subject to strict regulation by the Swiss authorities. JML represents the BankSwiss, SwissPlus, and SwissGold programs discussed in this book.

All staff members are fluent in English and understand the special concerns of the international investor. They know about all the many little details that are critical to you as a non-Swiss investor and have answers to your tax questions and other legalities. Contact the company at:

JML Jurg M. Lattmann AG
Swiss Investment Counsellors
Baarerstrasse 53, Dept. 212
CH-6304 Zug, Switzerland

When you contact a Swiss insurance broker, in addition to your name, address, and telephone number, be sure to include your date of birth, marital status, citizenship, number of children and their ages, name of spouse, and a clear definition of your financial objectives, including what dollar amount you would like to invest.

CHAPTER 10

GOLD AND
THE SWISS
METHOD OF
ACQUIRING IT

For thousands of years, gold has been man's premier store of value, more trusted worldwide by individuals than any paper investment or paper currency. Gold cannot be inflated by printing more of it. It cannot be devalued by government decree. And, unlike the case with paper currency or many other kinds of investments (such as stocks and bonds), gold is an asset that does not depend upon anybody's promise to repay.

Gold is one of the scarcest and thus most sought-after metals on earth. It cannot be fabricated by man, and nature limits its supply. Although gold has been mined for more than 6,000 years, only about 110,000 metric tons have ever been produced. If you could bring it all together, that is just enough to make a cube measuring only 18 meters (approximately 55 feet) along each side. The amount of new gold currently mined each year totals less than 2,000 metric tons, an amount that could be fit comfortably into the living room of a small house.

Gold is a traditional means of inflation protection. Some investors have been disappointed with the performance of gold in the past decade, but they are forgetting the primary purpose of gold as an inflation hedge. There has been very little inflation in the American economy in the past decade, so there has been nothing to be protected from. This does not mean that gold has been a bad investment. The proper comparison is not to the performance of other investments but to buying life insurance and not dying. The gold did exactly what it was supposed to do in the investor's portfolio—provided a store of value with inflation protection. An investor who is paying attention to the current price of gold is completely missing the point.

Gold is the most effective protection of purchasing power. This is illustrated by comparing its value today with its value in Biblical times. From the Old Testament we learn that during the reign of King Nebuchadnezzar of Babylonia, an ounce of gold bought 350 loaves of bread. An ounce of gold today will still buy about 350 loaves of bread.

Speculators have often lost badly with gold, but that is true of any speculation, and it is not because of some inherent characteristic of gold. This speculation is very different from the proper use of gold in an investment portfolio—as a way of achieving balance, diversification, and inflation insurance.

To put an entire savings program into diversified paper investments without a gold diversification is not a truly balanced plan. The security of the Swiss franc is one step in that diversification because of its strong gold backing and traditional strength as a currency. But it is only a step. The next step is to diversify some of the portfolio into a pure gold investment.

(In deciding how much of a portfolio should go to each type of investment, it is best to ignore the existence of the personal residence or a personally owned business. These are not really investment assets and serve a different purpose. They do not provide ready access to capital for either growth or emergency funds. To achieve a properly balanced portfolio, it is better to diversify based on only the liquid investments. Otherwise one can find that the picture has become unbalanced by including a very large part of the wealth in a nonliquid position and counting that as part of the diversification.)

Every paper currency buys less than it did at the turn of the century, but gold buys almost two times more. That is true inflation insurance, and it has nothing to do with overnight speculations on a belief in short-term price trends. There is nothing wrong with speculation, but it should not be confused with balancing a portfolio. In fact, a small percentage of any diversified portfolio is devoted to speculation.

As we have seen in Chapter 1, paper money inevitably declines in value and purchasing power. In an era when most governments have legally freed themselves from any requirement to act responsibly or tie their paper to real assets, this makes it particularly important for the investor to create his own "reserve fund" since the government's paper money no longer is required to have one.

Gold has an international value that tends to respond to the changes in value of national currencies. Time and again, gold has proved a successful hedge against the devaluation of an investor's national currency.

Gold is one of the few investments that has survived—and even thrived—during times of economic uncertainty. It is man's classic hedge against almost any monetary crisis, moving independently of paper investments. For example, in the slump following the "Wall Street Crash," from September 1929 to April 1932, the Dow Jones Industrial

Index slid from 382 to 56—a drop in value of 85 percent—and some 4,000 U.S. banks closed their doors. Meanwhile, the price of gold actually went up.

Gold also increased in value during the events following "Black Monday," October 19, 1987, when the Morgan Stanley index of world shares fell 19 percent in 10 days. And during the mini-crashes that have afflicted the stock markets since then, gold has held its value and ignored the travails of share investment. This is why so many investors worldwide see gold as the "ultimate asset"—an important and secure part of their investment portfolios.

INVESTING IN GOLD BULLION COINS

Although many numismatic gold coins have been purchased by investors, most investors think of gold bullion coins when they think of investing in "gold coins." And bullion coins are favored by many investors who want physical possession of their gold. The popularity of these coins and privately minted coinlike medallions can be attributed to their small size, convenient weights, and ease of storage.

The "typical" gold bullion coin is legal tender of a nation, and its gold content is guaranteed by the issuing nation. It bears a face value that is largely symbolic, because its market value depends totally on its gold content.

If you invest in gold bullion coins or in privately issued coinlike gold medallions, pieces, or "rounds," it will be easy for you to keep track of the daily value of your holdings because many of the most popular gold bullion coins and medallions contain one troy ounce of pure gold, and the price of an ounce of gold is reported daily in most newspapers.

Other bullion coins have been minted in easy fractional weights such as 1/2 ounce, 1/4 ounce, and 1/10 ounce. Among the countries issuing bullion coins are

South Africa, Canada, Mexico, China, Great Britain, and the United States.

Bullion coins normally sell for a 3 to 15 percent premium over the bullion value of gold, but a large part of this premium may be recovered at resale. The premium of gold coins is justified by their ready divisibility, convenience, portability, and marketability.

While many gold investors would prefer to keep all of their gold coins at home or nearby, other strategists keep only enough coins for immediate needs after a political or civil disaster and the cost of tickets for the entire family to get to Switzerland, and keep the rest of their coins in a secure arrangement with a Swiss bank.

One of the best sources for gold coins and bullion is a firm founded in 1982 by two of the former senior officers of Deak-Perera, at the time the nation's oldest and largest precious metals and foreign exchange firm. International Financial Consultants Inc. (Suite 400A, 1700 Rockville Pike, Rockville, MD, 20852) is not a "coin dealer," meaning that it does not take positions in the precious metals, therefore creating a bias to sell certain items. Instead, through its domestic and international network of wholesalers it buys and sells at competitive prices. International Financial Consultants can be called in the United States and Canada on a toll-free line (800-831-0007) for current market quotes or general information.

Clients and friends of the firm receive a monthly newsletter, *Information Line*, free of charge. The publication will keep you up-to-date on the precious metals and foreign exchange markets.

International Financial Consultants is well known in the financial newsletter industry and at one time or another has been recognized as a "recommended vendor" by many writers in the financial newsletter industry. The principals, Michael Checkan and Glen Kirsch, have been in the precious metals/foreign exchange business for a combined total of 50 years.

GOLD ACCUMULATION PLANS—
AN ECONOMICAL WAY TO ENJOY OWNERSHIP

Gold accumulation programs allow the investor to enjoy all the benefits of investing in gold without the responsibilities and costs of handling and storage. An accumulation plan is an organized method of buying gold purely for its investment and inflation-insurance aspects and does not involve gambling on coin values or other gimmicks. And it is designed to be more efficient and more economical than buying gold coins for their bullion value.

A monthly accumulation plan is based on cost-averaging rather than trying to outguess the market. It is designed for simple and systematic savings. For example, an investor might decide to put $250 per month into gold. That $250 is going into gold every month, regardless of what the market does. In the long run, the gold's cost will be less than the average market price in the same period. This is called cost-averaging. It requires no market expertise from the investor, just the dedication to make the same fixed investment each month regardless of the market. (In fact, some investors make a point of *not* looking at the market price.)

A similar technique is used by stock market investors—the cost-averaging principle is the same regardless of what is being bought. A fixed dollar amount is being invested every month rather than buying a fixed unit such as one share or one ounce.

Buying gold through accumulation programs can provide you with a number of advantages. You can make purchases at any time. Your order will be combined with other orders received that same day and will be executed the next business day. Since your brokerage house or bank buys and sells in the wholesale bullion dealer market, you are assured of competitive prices.

Because you are investing by the dollar amount and not by the ounce, your purchases are made in whole or partial ounces. And you pay discounted commission rates that are up to 40 percent less than what a regular broker charges for transactions.

Your gold is stored in major depositories and is fully insured. Your record keeping is done for you, and you will receive a confirmation of each transaction and a periodic summary statement. While you leave your gold in an accumulation program, you do not have to pay state or local taxes.

You can liquidate your accumulation plan holdings at any time. And when you do decide to sell, you will avoid paying costly assaying fees for weight and purity testing.

SWISSGOLD—
THE SWISS GOLD ACCUMULATION METHOD

SwissGold is an investment account created by UeberseeBank (also the creator of BankSwiss, as discussed on page 39). The bank does not engage in general commercial banking or in lending to corporations or foreign governments, so it is not exposed to such risks, nor does it have any conflicts of interest with managing the investors' money for best results.

UeberseeBank handles the SwissGold accounts, sending detailed statements on each purchase of gold made for the investor. By purchasing in this manner, the investors benefit from the bank's being able to buy at wholesale prices normally available only to large purchasers. In turn, the investor does not pay an extra fee on small unit amounts or the regular spread charged when buying and selling gold. These savings can be as much as 3 percent because of the wholesale price and another 8 percent by not having to pay small order surcharges. When added to the 20 percent savings that is often typical with cost-averaging, the investor is able to build the gold portion of his portfolio in the most economical way.

Naturally, such accounts are treated with the same secrecy as any other Swiss bank account. Each investor's gold is held separately by the bank in a fiduciary (trustee) relationship. This is important, because it means that the gold is always the investor's property and not merely a gold-denominated obligation of the bank. Thus solvency or credit standing of the bank cannot affect the investor's holdings, although a bank failure in Switzerland is almost unimaginable even with a commercial bank—and UeberseeBank does not even assume commercial risks. Of course, the gold is insured as well as guarded, and the investor has a choice of having it stored in Switzerland, the United States, or Canada.

SwissGold accounts can be tailored to the investor's needs. Account possibilities range from monthly purchases to large lump sum purchases. One may want to invest more money to achieve the diversification goal more quickly than originally intended, and the investor can suspend monthly purchases at any time without penalty. Flexibility is the keyword in the operation of these accounts.

Further information on SwissGold is available from the creator of the program:

JML Jurg M. Lattmann AG
Swiss Investment Counsellors
Baarerstrasse 53, Dept. 212
CH-6304 Zug, Switzerland

CHAPTER 11

FORMING
A SWISS
COMPANY

Switzerland is not a tax haven in the sense that one might form a company in a zero-tax country such as Bermuda or the Cayman Islands. But in some circumstances it does have its uses as a place to incorporate.

Switzerland has a special tax treatment for holding companies. This special treatment applies also to ordinary companies to the extent that they operate as holding companies and derive income from merely "passive" sources (dividends, interest, etc.). Such tax exemptions are highly limited, however; for instance, they do not apply to interest from loans and royalties from leases paid by companies in which one has stock ownership. Still, a pure holding company pays no federal income tax, only a federal capital tax on the value of share capital and a similar canton capital tax.

Domiciliary companies (those based in Switzerland but doing business outside the country) have been granted exemptions from local income taxes by some cantons. The applicable taxes are reduced cantonal capital tax, federal income tax, and federal capital tax.

ADVANTAGES OF A SWISS COMPANY

The legalities of forming a company in Switzerland are fairly simple, with the concept of freedom of trade and commerce invoked in most cases. All persons, including foreigners, are held to have the constitutional right to establish a business and/or engage in business activity.

Many people like to form a Swiss company as a holding company, particularly for nonproducing assets, such as a vacation home in the Caribbean, on the assumption that the Swiss neutrality of the registered ownership may protect them should a local government ever start confiscating American property. This theory gained momentum after the Cuban revolution, when American property was seized without compensation but Swiss property was not. This type of use of a Swiss company avoids tax issues, since the company has no income, and therefore both Swiss income tax and Swiss withholding tax on dividends are irrelevant. An investor can even execute nominee agreements with his Swiss company, making the investor the beneficial owner and the Swiss company in effect a private trustee. This is particularly useful for property such as a vacation home or yacht, which carries liability risks that a bank trust department would be unwilling to handle in the bank's own name.

(Forming a Swiss company does not provide a way around the Swiss real estate ownership requirements, as discussed in Chapter 16 on buying a vacation home in

Switzerland. For local real estate purchases, the Swiss authorities do inquire into the beneficial ownership of a company.)

A Swiss company might also be useful if one wants a Swiss image but the company is going to earn little if any money. An intriguing recent example of this was a large British food company that wanted to market a new bread with a gourmet image and price. Once it decided on a suitable trademark, it formed a Swiss company to own the British trademark rights and then had the Swiss company license the use of the trademarks to its British parent. What this did was let the company place a label on the bread saying "Made under license from XYZ Bakers, Alpine Village, Switzerland," thus implying an impressive pedigree to customers.

COMPANY NAMES AND FORMATION

For the most part, Swiss law allows freedom of choice when naming a new company. However, the name must clearly indicate the structure of the firm. Typical legal structures include single owner, partnership, company limited by shares, or cooperative. The name must not be misleading, and geographical designations are not permitted. Thus you will not be able to use Swiss or Switzerland or Zurich or Geneva in the name. (There are a few exceptions for major enterprises like Swissair.)

A firm's entry into the Register of Commerce (also known as the Commercial Register) creates a certain amount of legal protection as well as obligations. Among these are protection against infringement on the firm name, an obligation for the firm to maintain books of account, and subjection to bankruptcy proceedings and special proceedings to enforce payment of bills and exchange. (The Register of Commerce performs functions that in the United States would be done by the state commissions that oversee corporations and by county offices that record deeds.)

All Register entries must contain the name of the firm; the firm's domicile; the owner's name, if a single-owner firm; the partners' names of a general or limited partnership; and, in the case of limited liability companies, the amount up to which the principals are liable. In the case of a corporation, the amount of capital stock must be entered along with the shares' nominal value, the names of management and board of director personnel, and the names of persons with the authority to sign or act on behalf of the corporation.

Entries concerning the location of the firm's head office are also made in the Register. Branch offices are registered at their locations as well as at the locations of their head offices. Cantonal authorities keep the Register, subject to the supervision of the Federal Office of the Register of Commerce.

Formation of a company in Switzerland will usually take about two weeks.

TYPES OF COMPANIES AVAILABLE

Swiss business enterprises are allowed in such forms as:

1. *The single-owner firm*, or sole proprietorship.
2. *The general partnership*, which is an association of two or more individuals. It has unlimited liability to the creditors of the organization. It can be formed under a firm mandate for the purpose of operating a trading enterprise, an industrial enterprise, or other enterprise that is based on commercial principles. The contract of partnership, written as a result of such a business alliance, must be entered in the Register of Commerce. Although not considered a corporate body, the general partnership can acquire rights, assume liabilities, institute legal action, and sue or be sued.

3.   *The limited partnership.* Must have at least one general partner but with one or more partners who have limited liability and no voice in management.

4.   *The corporation.* This is the legal form most often used to incorporate holding and investment companies. It is considered the best legal form for an enterprise that participates in foreign business interests.

5.   *The limited partnership corporation.* Not often encountered, it has some characteristics of both the corporation and the limited partnership. Under the limited partnership corporation, one or more persons may assume management of an enterprise as partners (in the case of more than one person) with full liability to creditors. In order for such an entity to raise additional capital, limited liability shares are offered for subscription. This is a recognized legal form in Switzerland.

6.   *The limited liability company.* This is an association of two or more persons or companies with a firm name and fixed capital, having its own legal personality. Each partner contributes a fixed amount of capital; however, this capital is not considered the same as a joint stock company share. The registered capital of such a company must be at least 20,000 francs, but not more than 2,000,000 francs, and each partner may, in certain cases prescribed by law, be held liable for up to this amount (in excess of his own capital contribution). When the company is formed, each partner must pay at least 50 percent of his capital contribution, either as cash or noncash capital. Thus, the limited liability company may be considered a hybrid of a joint stock company and a personal partnership. However, it is not often encountered in Switzerland since it does not provide any specific advantages over the regular corporation (as does the German GmbH in Germany).

For a foreign investor wishing to use a Swiss entity to hold an asset, however, the limited liability company may offer several advantages. There are no requirements for compulsory auditors, a Swiss-majority board of directors, or managers to be Swiss, though a company must have at least one manager resident in Switzerland. For an inactive property-holding company, the avoidance of an annual audit fee alone is a significant savings.

Despite these advantages, the limited liability company is rarely encountered, and Swiss lawyers will generally try to sell the investor on the more familiar corporation.

7. *The Swiss cooperative.* Structured much like the corporation, it usually consists of several persons or companies with the primary purpose of promoting and protecting the business interests of its members. The capital is not fixed in advance, and unless the bylaws state otherwise, its liabilities are limited to its own assets.

8. *The ordinary partnership.* This is a loose form of organization, usually created to serve a specific pur-pose. It is not entered in the Commercial Register. Essentially, it is a contract of association, outlining the joint and several liabilities of the partners. It does not assume a separate firm name.

THE CORPORATION

The Swiss legal entity known as the corporation is a company with its own firm name. Its capital is divided into shares, and its liabilities are exclusively covered by its assets.

The minimum allowable capitalization of a Swiss corporation is 50,000 francs, at least 20,000 francs of which must be paid in cash or provided in subscription by noncash capital at the time of incorporation. In the case of fully paid-up capital stock, the corporation can issue either registered or bearer shares; if the capital stock is not paid up, the corporation can issue only registered shares. The par value of a share must be at least 100 francs. The "no par value" share is nonexistent under Swiss law.

At least three prospective shareholders are required for forming a Swiss corporation. If one of the shareholders wants to remain unidentified, he may, under certain conditions, have a third party subscribe as his trustee.

Corporation bylaws must contain provisions relative to:

1. The firm name.
2. The location of the head office.
3. The number and par value of the registered shares of capital stock and the bearer shares of capital stock.
4. The time, place, frequency, etc., of the shareholder's meetings.
5. The board of directors, auditor, and forms of notification.

The corporation is organized through a general meeting of shareholders, the board of directors, and auditors.

The functions of the shareholders' meetings are to approve the profit and loss account; to approve the balance sheet and the annual report; to adopt resolutions concerning the distribution of net profits, especially as it applies to the declaration of dividends; to elect directors and auditors; to approve board of directors' actions to amend the bylaws of the constitution; and to determine liquidation procedures.

The board of directors is made up of one member or several members, all of whom must be shareholders. If there is only one director, he must be a Swiss national living in Switzerland. If the board of directors consists of several persons, the majority must be of Swiss nationality and live in Switzerland. The board's activities are outlined in the bylaws of the corporation's constitution, which must be written in accordance with Swiss law.

One or several auditors are elected at the shareholders' meeting. Auditors are not required to be shareholders. The auditors may be individuals or corporate entities, such as a fiduciary company or an auditing association.

MOVING A FOREIGN CORPORATION TO SWITZERLAND

When a foreign corporation transfers to Switzerland, the question of liquidation and reestablishment must be decided. Generally, the bylaws of a corporation set forth its domicile. The bylaws must be written in accordance with the national law that applies to corporations. Thus, if the laws of the country where the corporation is originally formed are such that transference to another country implies liquidation, then liquidation, before subsequent reestablishment in the new domicile, is mandatory. Likewise, if the laws of the country to which the corporation is being transferred specifically state the necessity of reincorporation, liquidation and reestablishment would be mandatory. However, under such circumstances, the Federal Council of Switzerland is authorized to grant permission to a corporation to transfer to Switzerland without prior liquidation, subject to the following provisions:

1. The corporation must prove that, according to the laws of the country where it was formed, it had a legal personality.
2. The figures of the most current, approved balance sheet must indicate that the capital stock is fully covered by assets.
3. The transfer of the corporation's domicile must have been validated through a resolution, in accordance

with the bylaws.

If the Federal Council refuses permission to a foreign corporation to redomicile in Switzerland without prior liquidation, the corporation must liquidate and reincorporate in Switzerland in order to acquire legal status there. This reestablishment is called "qualified incorporation," and it must be accompanied by a transfer of assets and liabilities to the corporation's Swiss domicile. If the Federal Council permits such a transfer, entry of the corporation in the Register of Commerce is required, and its bylaws must be adapted to Swiss law within six months. In the case of one delay, the Federal Council may grant an extension of time; if the second term elapses before the necessary constitutional revisions are made, its entry in the Register of Commerce is officially canceled.

ESTABLISHING A BRANCH
OFFICE IN SWITZERLAND

If a foreign corporation wishes to establish a branch office in Switzerland, Swiss law presupposes that a head office of the corporation is domiciled elsewhere. A foreign corporation cannot establish a Swiss branch in anticipation of isolating it from Swiss commerce and Swiss law. This means that if it is to protect its business operations, the branch must adapt to Swiss rules and regulations. The following principles must be adhered to:

1. The admission, existence, and activities of a foreign branch in Switzerland are regulated by Swiss law.
2. Entry in the Register of Commerce by the Swiss branch of a foreign corporation is required in exactly the same manner as that of a Swiss firm.
3. The Swiss branch of the foreign corporation is obliged by Swiss law to keep books of account and prepare financial statements periodically.

4.   The branch office must be represented by an author-
      ized person of Swiss residence.

Rules for establishing a branch office in Switzerland
must be followed when the actual administration of a corporation is transferred to Switzerland and its center of
operation remains in the foreign domicile. If, however,
the center of operation also transfers to Switzerland, the
rules for transferring a corporation are effective.

Insofar as Swiss law is concerned, the expenses
incurred in forming a corporation are the stamp duty
levied on the newly issued shares, the fees for entry in the
Register of Commerce, and the cost of the notarized certificate of incorporation. Additional expenses might
include fees for an attorney or other qualified counsel to
aid and advise you in establishing the corporation, and
the appointing of a director, who must be paid for his
services. The cost depends, of course, upon the activity
and complexity of the enterprise. Special, more mundane
services such as maintaining an office, bookkeeping, tax
accounting, and general correspondence also have to be
paid for. For on-the-spot advice and assistance in the
forming of a Swiss corporation, contact a Swiss lawyer or
a Swiss bank.

CHAPTER 12

TAXATION

Switzerland has a somewhat complex system of taxation. Due to its structure, taxes are levied concurrently by three different authorities: the federal government, the cantons, and the municipalities. Generally speaking, the Swiss federal tax laws are uniform throughout the country, but the laws of the cantons and municipalities may differ. Therefore, tax rules and tax liabilities are likely to vary from one place to another.

In principle, Swiss companies are taxed at the three levels—federal, cantonal, and municipal—on their profit and capital. However, the rates as well as the methods of taxation differ according to the firm's legal structure. Although Swiss civil law acknowledges only one form of joint stock company, there are three different forms in terms of fiscal treatment: the operating company, the holding company, and the domiciliary company.

An operating company is one that engages in an industrial, manufacturing, or service activity. Such a company is liable for a federal tax called a defense tax, plus taxes on net earnings, capital stock, and open and undisclosed reserves. Stamp duties amount to 2 percent of the paid-in capital stock.

Swiss law defines a holding company as one whose main purpose is to participate in other companies through investments. The holding company is almost always legally structured as a corporation. The Swiss federal tax system, as well as those of most of the cantons, grants holding companies certain tax privileges:

1. The regular tax is reduced.
2. The taxable capital is computed on a reduced basis.
3. In lieu of options one and two, a proportional tax on capital, in combination with a tax exemption on earnings, is applicable.

However, for the Swiss holding company to gain tax privileges offered by the federal tax system, it must meet the requirements outlined by federal tax regulations. Otherwise, the federal tax system treats the holding company the same as an operating company.

The domiciliary company has its legal domicile in Switzerland but has no office space. It does not engage in business activities in Switzerland. Such a company is usually limited by shares.

The domiciliary company is often established in lieu of a holding company when the requirements for a holding company cannot be met. Domiciliary companies are often sales agencies or patent and/or copyright marketing companies.

Any tax benefits to the domiciliary company come

from the canton. The federal tax system does not recognize it but taxes it as an operating company (if certain conditions are met, the federal system may grant the domiciliary company similar deductions to that of the holding company). Concerning canton taxation, the pure domiciliary company enjoys more extensive tax advantages than the so-called mixed company; however, variations on the domiciliary company do obtain some tax advantages in the cantons. Shareholder dividends paid by the domiciliary company are subject to a withholding tax that is currently 35 percent.

WITHHOLDING TAX

The Swiss impose a 35 percent withholding tax on interest paid by a Swiss payor. You can recover this money by the simple expedient of declaring the interest to the IRS. You can either obtain a refund from the Swiss after getting the proper forms certified by the IRS, or you can apply the amount as a credit on your U.S. taxes under the foreign tax credit rules. Note that this is a credit, not a deduction, so it comes right off the amount of the check you would have paid to the IRS. However, the Swiss do not issue 1099 forms, and it may be difficult to determine the appropriate exchange rate for the dollar, although the IRS eventually gets around to printing an official rate for the preceding year.

One way to avoid the withholding tax is to have a fiduciary account instead of a regular bank account. This is really the equivalent of having the trust department of an American bank handle your investments instead of putting the money in a CD. More information on fiduciary accounts is given in Chapter 13. All of the investments are made outside of Switzerland, in whatever manner you instruct the bank—mortgages, mutual funds, or other banks. The money is merely passing through Switzerland and is not taxed there.

SWISS
BANK
SERVICES

Though Switzerland's banking system has a cen-
turies-old heritage of secrecy, that heritage was not put
into law until 1934. In effect, the Swiss opted to hold on
to their secrecy while other banking systems around the
world were beginning to compromise. In the 1930s, many
other nations, including the United States, were creating
a distinction between deposit banks and investment
banks, but the Swiss legislature refused to follow that
trend. The Swiss opted to retain "universal" banking, or
full-service type banking, which means that your Swiss
bank can be a deposit bank, a checking account bank, a
stockbroker, a commercial lender, an investment bank—
everything you need.

Swiss banks as a whole are very safe, and they take the necessary measures to regulate the entirety of their industry so that Swiss banking does not lose any of its reputation for sound money management. In addition to the formal requirements imposed by the Banking Act of 1934 and strict supervision by the Banking Commission, Swiss banks are also subjected to regular audits. The first audit is to comply with the Swiss corporation law, which every Swiss corporation must undergo. The second is the banking audit, which must be conducted by one of 17 firms that have been specially approved by the Banking Commission to conduct bank audits. Over the years, these bank audits have become very complex and exacting. The audit firms have a whole set of detailed rules by which they go over the bank's books.

The audit has become the primary guarantee for the legal protection of Swiss bank depositors. The banks and the 17 audit firms actually supervise and regulate banking in Switzerland to a far greater extent than governments regulate banking in other nations.

The banking law also requires stiff liquidity and capital requirements for the operation of a Swiss bank. These are among the most rigid in the world. The liquidity formula is rather complicated, but the end product is that most private Swiss banks have liquidity at or around 100 percent, which is unprecedented in other national banking systems. The formula for capital requirements in Swiss banks means that around 7 to 9 percent of total liabilities must be equity. This is a high percentage in relation to other countries. Swiss banks that own securities must write them down to market or cost (whichever is lower) every month so no Swiss bank will have unrealized paper losses on its securities, as often happens to banks in other countries.

Swiss commercial banks adhere closely to policies established by banks throughout the world. From the purely local viewpoint, Swiss credit policies apply to virtually all types of loans; however, credit extended to foreign customers is limited to top-ranking companies and to the financing of exports from Switzerland. Loan terms vary with such factors as the value of collateral but are generally more favorable in Switzerland than in many other countries.

To a large extent, the amount of bank credit that a company can get depends upon how much confidence the company can generate in the banker's mind; therefore, each individual case is subject to different treatment. To this end, a typical, business-oriented Swiss bank goes to considerable trouble to analyze its clients' needs and provide solutions that are fitting to the capital requirements of each case. To customers domiciled in Switzerland, the following services are typically offered:

1. Short-term credit of all kinds, whether secured or unsecured. This may be in current account form or as a fixed advance in either Swiss francs or foreign currency.
2. Mortgage loans.
3. Leasing and factoring.
4. Refinancing of leasing operations.
5. The discounting of acceptances, including the financing of medium-term receivables, that result from the export business.
6. The opening of letters of credit.
7. Guarantees, sureties, and bonds for public authorities and/or private persons.

To further broaden their scope in the world money market, Swiss banks place the following facilities at the service of Swiss-domiciled clients:

1. Direct short- to medium-term loans, which may be in Swiss francs or other convertible currencies, on fixed interest or a roll-over basis.

2. Financing of Swiss merchandise (together with an export risk guarantee by the Swiss government).

3. "Bridging" loans as a means of preliminary financing prior to capital market transactions in Switzerland and on the Euromarket.

The banks of Switzerland not only assist corporations in specialized ways but business and private clients as well. Advice or other services through some banks include:

1. Transfer of payments in the national and international sectors.
2. Buying and selling bank notes and paying instruments in foreign currencies.
3. Negotiation of stock market transactions internally and abroad.
4. Securities management and custody.
5. Establishment of trusts and counseling in investments.

Extremely sensitive to and knowledgeable of business and commerce conditions in Switzerland, Swiss banks help clients establish contacts necessary to launch a Swiss enterprise. Some publish brochures and booklets containing detailed information on economic and business conditions. Such publications also provide information on special features of specific regional industries. Some major banks have branches throughout Switzerland as well as in London, Tokyo, New York, Luxembourg, and Panama. The typical major Swiss bank has representation in most major financial centers and can be in continuous communications with thousands of correspondent banks worldwide.

CHAPTER 14

USE AN OFFSHORE CORPORATION OR TRUST TO HOLD SWISS INVESTMENTS

It is important to remember that Switzerland is a money-management center, not a tax haven. Swiss residents, including corporations, do pay fairly substantial income taxes. For this reason, many investors seeking to have an investment portfolio actively managed from Switzerland prefer to have that portfolio owned by a trust or corporation based in a tax haven.

The most popular investments for U.S. investors in recent years have been mutual funds and insurance products. For the internationally minded investor, there are offshore versions of these products available. In many cases, they offer even more benefits to U.S. investors than do their domestic counterparts. The IRS and other elements of the

U.S. government apparently do not believe in offering international opportunities to U.S. citizens, however, so in some cases, these investments are less attractive to U.S. investors than to residents of other countries.

The main obstacle standing in the way of many foreign opportunities is U.S. securities laws. Any "investment contract" sold in the United States must be registered with the federal Securities and Exchange Commission (SEC) and its counterpart in each of the states. This is a very expensive process. U.S. securities laws require far more disclosure than do those of most foreign countries and also require different accounting practices. Therefore, many offshore mutual fund companies decide that whatever income they might eventually earn would be inadequate compensation for the time and expense involved in attempting to comply with U.S. securities laws. In fact, several of the mutual funds and hedge funds with the top performance records are run from the United States by U.S. residents but do not accept investments from U.S. residents. To reduce registration costs and avoid other restrictions, the funds are made available only to foreigners. That doesn't mean that there is something dirty or illegal about them; it merely means that the funds are not registered for sale in the United States.

Successful foreign funds don't need the American market and see little reason to pay the outrageous fees brought about by our litigious society. (For a similar reason, some of the best foreign cars cannot be purchased in the United States—the makers of $100,000 custom cars are not about to give the federal government 10 free cars per year for destruction testing.) Some of the funds cannot meet U.S. legal requirements because they charge investors a performance fee rather than a management fee based on a percentage of assets. But many investors would actually prefer a fund manager whose only compensation is a share of the profits instead of a fee based on the total investments in the fund. The manager's goals are different.

Fortunately, U.S. citizens can get around the obstacles through bank accounts or trusts. It is not illegal for Americans to buy offshore mutual funds (called "unit trusts" in some countries) or any other security that is not registered for sale in the United States. Basically, you can travel overseas to buy the shares in person, open a foreign bank account and invest through the account, or establish a foreign trust. Only then will these opportunities be open to you.

Creating a foreign irrevocable trust that in turn owns a foreign corporation has proven a viable solution in some circumstances. Recently revised SEC regulations also make it legal for such a corporation to purchase foreign shares and funds that could not be purchased by an American directly. Regulation S now defines circumstances in which such purchases may be made by a corporation indirectly controlled by an American shareholder (such as control through an asset-protection trust). In many cases, such a trust and corporation structure can be created in a way that provides both asset protection and fully legal income-tax exemption for the trust or corporation.

One of the best sources of help in setting up offshore trusts and corporations is an American certified accountant who has a large practice in Panama. Marc Harris holds a master's degree in business administration from Columbia University and completed the certified public accountancy examination at the age of 18. He is believed to be the youngest person in the United States to pass the examination.

He opened his Panamanian firm in 1985 after serving as a consultant with the accounting firm of Ernst & Whinney. His services are highly recommended because he is able to create and administer offshore corporations and trusts in complete compliance with U.S. laws. Often an American client uses a tax-haven-based advisor who knows the local laws but is not familiar with American tax law requirements and technicalities, and the client eventually gets into trouble. Marc Harris has a unique ability to bridge the two worlds for his clients. Although based in Panama, he can create and administer corporations and trusts that are registered in all of the popular tax havens.

The Harris Organization is the Panamanian representative for Charles Schwab Discount Brokerage, the Jardine Fleming Offshore Funds, JML Swiss Investment Counsellors, and other offshore products. For more information, write to:

The Harris Organization
Attn: Traditional Client Services
Estafeta El Dorado
Apartado Postal 6-1097
Panama 6, Panama

Purchasing a Swiss annuity or opening a SwissGold account can a safe do-it-yourself project, but if you decide on more active investing that requires a trust or corporation, this can only be done properly with quality professional advice. Only a detailed inspection of the specific situation with the aid of a competent professional can determine the precise approach to be followed.

For the best detailed information on tax havens, read *The Tax Haven Report*, published by Scope International Ltd., Box AS125, Forestside House, Forestside, Rowlands Castle, Hants., PO9 6EE, United Kingdom. The publisher will send a free catalog on request. And of course you'll want to read *Using Offshore Havens for Privacy and Profit* by Adam Starchild, published by Paladin Press, P.O. Box 1307, Boulder, CO, 80306.

Yet another source of information is Eden Press, which publishes a series of special reports on different havens and techniques by which Americans can use them. You can obtain this catalog free by writing to Eden at P.O. Box 8410, Fountain Valley, CA, 92728.

If you want to gain a good understanding of how the government views tax havens, University Microfilms International, through its Books On Demand program, is now making available *Tax Havens and Their Uses by United States Taxpayers* by Richard Gordon. Frequently referred to as "The Gordon Report," this is a 1981 U.S. Treasury Department study prepared at the request of Congress. It gives considerable detail and examples of the uses of tax havens. It is available from University Microfilms for $67.30 softbound or $73.30 hardbound. Out of print for over a decade, it still contains much useful information for anyone interested in tax havens. Copies can be ordered through booksellers or directly from:

University Microfilms International
300 North Zeeb Road
Ann Arbor, MI 48106-1346

The UMI catalog number of the book is AU00435, and UMI accepts Visa or MasterCard.

Just stop and think for a moment how much faster your money can grow if you are not paying out an average of 40 percent to a taxing government somewhere.

CHAPTER 15

PORTFOLIO MANAGEMENT FROM A SWISS BASE

Portfolio management by an independent investment advisory firm is an alternative to having a Swiss
bank manage an investment account, such as is offered by
UeberseeBank in its BankSwiss program. Such an independent Swiss firm can manage your investment account
whether it be an individual portfolio or a portfolio for
your offshore trust or corporation.

A new asset-management and international financial consulting company was opened by Hans Weber and
his partners in Zurich in 1992. Some readers may remember Weber from his Deak-Perera days, when he ran
Foreign Commerce Bank (FOCOBANK) in Switzerland
for almost 30 years as president and CEO. He decided to

leave the bank and establish his own firm after too many shareholder changes and mergers.

He was joined by Robert Vrijhof, formerly vice-president and head of FOCOBANK's portfolio management group, and Adrian Hartmann, formerly head of FOCO-BANK's North American subsidiary in Vancouver. The partners have a very sound and efficient asset-management operation providing very personalized service to their clientele.

The partners chose Bank Julius Baer in Zurich as the custodial bank for their clientele. Bank Julius Baer is one of the premier private banks in all of Switzerland. The 100-year-old family bank is safe, with a strong capital base of more than 40 billion Swiss francs under direct or indirect asset management.

Weber is a very conservative Swiss banker who adheres to strict, sound asset-management principles. His partners, Vrijhof and Hartmann, have the same investment philosophy. Their highest priority is the protection of long-term purchasing power. They provide a very personal, comprehensive financial service to a select group of private investors, and everything they do is customized to suit the particular needs of their clientele.

There are many advantages to using independent asset managers such as Weber and his partners rather than just relying on a Swiss bank. For example:

- Independent asset managers derive their income from an agreed-to percentage of the value of the client's funds under management. Therefore, the more profit the client makes, the more the asset manager makes. This is very different from dealing directly with a bank, which makes its money from brokerage and administrative fees.
- European asset managers understand the needs of North American clientele who use the dollar as their reference currency. Since Weber founded the firm,

the partners have advised North American clients to diversify a certain amount of their wealth out of the dollar. The funds have been invested in "hard currencies" such as the Swiss franc, German mark, French franc, and Dutch guilder.

The minimum amount to set up an account with this firm is US$250,000 or the equivalent in another currency. When you are ready to proceed, you can contact:

Weber, Hartmann, Vrijhof & Partners Ltd.
Attn: New Clients Department
Zurichstrasse 110B
8134 Adllswil
Switzerland

CHAPTER 16

BUYING A VACATION OR RETIREMENT HOME IN SWITZERLAND

Switzerland is a postcard-pretty paradise located at the peak of Europe. Gingerbread chalets laced with flower boxes are surrounded by rolling meadows. And above the whole of the country soar jagged, snow-covered peaks. Tidy streets wander through orderly towns filled with well-mannered people.

Switzerland's spectacular scenery draws people from around the world. Most educated Swiss speak some English, and Swiss health facilities are excellent. Furthermore, Switzerland is centrally located, a perfect hub for exploring Europe (sharing borders with France, Italy, Austria, Germany, and Liechtenstein). And it is politically and economically stable.

Switzerland is a safe, prosperous country with little crime, reliable and efficient public services, and virtually no unemployment or poverty. And if you're looking for recreation and healthy living, this is the place to come. Switzerland offers cross-country and downhill skiing, hiking, ice skating, therapeutic hot springs, and boating.

One of Switzerland's disadvantages is that it is land-locked and can be dull. Another is that it is expensive. Lunch in an average big-city cafe costs 15 to 20 Swiss francs (with 1 Swiss franc worth around 80 U.S. cents). A bottle of beer at a disco goes for SFr12. A Coke is about SFr4.5. And mineral water in a cafe will cost you SFr3.3! Prices are lower in small towns and during the off-season, but they are still quite high by American standards.

Because Switzerland attracts so many foreigners, the Swiss have constructed bureaucratic barriers to pro-tect their land from overdevelopment. It is extremely dif-ficult to obtain permanent residency in Switzerland. And foreigners cannot buy property in many areas, including Geneva, Lausanne, Gland, and Rolle. Gstaad, St. Moritz, Davos, Saanen, Schonried, and Zermatt have blocked property sales to nonresident foreigners.

Immigration as it is known in the United States does not exist in Switzerland. A visa is not required for stays of up to three months. After three months, you can apply to the local police for a one-year residency permit, which can be extended indefinitely with an annual application to the canton. After you have been a resident of Switzerland for five years, you can apply for a permanent domicile permit. These permits are contingent upon sub-stantial means or sought-after skills. Consult a Swiss lawyer for more detailed information.

To retire permanently in Switzerland, you must be 60 or older, have a yearly income of $20,000 from sources other than regular employment, no longer be employed by anyone, and have an "interest in Switzerland." The fourth stipulation is left deliberately vague to allow discretion in deciding difficult cases. You are most likely to be allowed to reside in Switzerland permanently if you have relatives in the country or have lived there for at least one year.

As an American retiree living in Switzerland, you are exempt from taxes on dividends and interest income originating from the United States. However, if your principal residence or business is in Switzerland, you are subject to federal, cantonal, and municipal taxes. The amount of these taxes varies. For example, while residents of Vaud Canton pay a 13 percent cantonal tax on SFr50,000, residents of Zug pay only a 7 percent cantonal tax on the same amount. The highest cantonal and local taxes are in Vaud, Geneva, Berne, and Lucerne; the lowest are in Zug, Zurich, and Graubunden.

In general, income taxes in Switzerland are comparable to those in the United States. The federal government levies an additional income tax ranging from 0.31 percent on incomes of SFr30,000 to 4.3 percent on incomes of SFr100,000 and up. Usually, cantons with the lowest income tax rates have the highest housing costs.

As a foreigner, you need permission from the government to buy land. It's possible but difficult for foreigners to buy land, a free-standing home, or an estate in rural areas; it's almost impossible to obtain permission to purchase property in cities such as Zurich and Geneva. In recreational regions, condominiums are the only properties readily available.

However, the laws are not nearly as limiting as they may seem, because many areas considered rural are within a few miles of ski resorts and spas. And the condos are attractive and spacious, many with traditional Swiss architecture, mountain views, and privacy.

Although foreigners cannot buy property in Gstaad, a small quota of properties in Rougemont in the canton of Vaud, only five minutes from Gstaad, is available to non-Swiss buyers.

Effective January 1, 1988, the new law Lex Fredreich changed the rules regarding foreign purchase of land in Switzerland. Previously, a Swiss developer could get advance authorization for a certain percentage of sales to foreigners. But now a developer must find a foreign prospective buyer first and then apply for permission to sell. This effectively stopped any new building for foreign purchase.

While availability of new construction has become tighter, resale of foreign-owned properties has become easier. Resale is controlled by the canton and is only possible after a 10-year period of ownership and with a demonstrated need to sell by the seller.

The Swiss government has overthrown many deals put together by Swiss attorneys using Swiss names or corporations to try to avoid the restrictions on foreign ownership, and I would recommend that you avoid such schemes.

Unless you have a Swiss residency permit, you cannot occupy your Swiss property for more than three months per calendar year. You can, however, arrive at the beginning of the last quarter of one year and depart at the end of the first quarter of the following year. This allows for a six-month stay.

Financing can be obtained, using the property as security, on 60 to 65 percent of the purchase price. And many banks offer 100 percent financing with the deposit of additional collateral. Rates are about 10 percent. It's usually possible to borrow back some of the equity at any time, using the arrangement as a limited line of credit.

Two of the most active real estate agents dealing with foreign buyers are:

Revac S.A.
Montbrillant 52
CH-1202 Geneva

Globe Plan S.A.
24 ave. Mon-Repos
CH-1005 Lausanne

Choose your piece of Switzerland according to the life-style you want. If you like to ski or hike, consider the Alps. If you're accustomed to big-city life, think about Zurich or Geneva. If you consider retirement a time to get away from the rat race, look into small towns or lakeside villages. Also consider what kind of culture would make you feel most at home. You can live in French, German, Italian, or Romansch Switzerland, depending upon your preference and knowledge of foreign languages. The Italian-speaking sections of Switzerland are the most open to foreigners and often the least expensive.

For visa information, contact the Embassy of Switzerland, 2900 Cathedral Ave. N.W., Washington, D.C., 20008. For general tourist information, contact the Swiss National Tourist Office, 608 Fifth Avenue, New York, NY, 10020.

CHAPTER 17

CAMPIONE:

Little Known
Tax-Free
Back Door to
Switzerland

Campione, on the shores of Lake Lugano, is distinguished by its uniqueness. It is a little piece of Italian soil completely surrounded by Switzerland. There are no border controls so there is complete freedom to pass in and out. It is located in the Swiss canton of Ticino, about 16 miles from the Italian border and 5 miles from Lugano by road. There are many recreational facilities in the immediate area, including golf, skiing, and water sports; Milan, with all of its cultural attractions, is only an hour away. Campione has about 2,000 inhabitants.

Campione's unique status has its origins in the thirteenth century when the village and its territory were presented by the Lord of Campione to the Church of St.

Ambrosius of Milan. This feudal property survived European upheavals and remained secure to the end of the eighteenth century, when it joined the new Cisalpine Republic. Afterward, Campione fell into Austria's hands for a short period until it was finally incorporated into the new Kingdom of Italy.

Economically, Campione belongs to Switzerland and uses Swiss banks and governmental facilities such as the post office, telephones, telegraphs, and traffic laws. Cars registered in Campione bear Swiss license plates.

Unlike in Switzerland, however, foreigners have no problem obtaining residency rights, so the enclave is enjoying a sudden popularity with people looking for a way to obtain Swiss residence. Having a house or apartment in Campione is all that is necessary to obtain a residence permit, although the local authorities do require that registered residents spend at least some time there. The lack of border controls gives Campione residents totally unrestricted access to all of Switzerland and Liechtenstein, so it can be a most valuable European executive base.

Besides its attraction as a residence, the enclave is also gaining in popularity because it has a unique tax haven status. Although part of Italy and subject to Italian law, there is no personal income tax and no municipal tax, as all of Campione's income is raised from the operation of a municipal casino. And residents are not subject to Switzerland's many double-taxation agreements with such countries as Canada, the United States, and most of western Europe. This makes Campione one of the world's most unique and least-known tax havens and a most attractive base for companies looking for a regional headquarters in Europe.

Companies formed in Campione have many advantages over Swiss companies, as they are able to use Swiss banking facilities and have a mailing address that appears Swiss, yet they are not subject to Switzerland's relatively high income and withholding taxes. They can be formed with a minimum capitalization of about $1,000 and, although formation takes longer than in Switzerland, a Campione company can be entirely owned and directed by foreigners. As a part of Italy, the European Union regulations apply to businesses, and this includes such things as the right to establish a business and residence by any citizen of another EU country. The formation is usually handled by Italian lawyers in Milan, and the fees are modest, since this is not a special or complex matter. The personal and company tax exemptions do not apply if the resident is doing business with Italy, but business with Italy can readily be done through a Swiss or Liechtenstein corporation as an intermediary.

Unlike in Switzerland, foreigners may buy real estate in Campione without restrictions, so acquisition of a site for a European regional headquarters is carried out with minimal red tape. Demand for real estate in Campione, however, has pushed prices well above the level of surrounding Ticino because there is so little of it. Apartments range from $2,500 to $3,500 per square yard, and you usually pay the broker a 3 percent buying commission on top of that (the seller also pays 3 percent).

The official language is, of course, Italian, and the enclave is in the Italian-speaking portion of Switzerland. Many international schools are located in Switzerland, so school arrangements for children of transferred executives can be made easily.

The recent referendum in which Swiss voters rejected an affiliation with the European Union means that Campione will retain its special value for some time to come. Without the free access to Switzerland that EU affiliation would have provided, the backdoor route via Campione will continue.

Getting started in Campione is much more difficult than in other tax havens because the enclave is not promoting itself. There is no central office of information to which one can turn for instant literature or other agents that you can write to for packets of nice brochures. You are not unwelcome, but nobody is going to go out of his way to let you in on this secret haven.

The only effective way to establish yourself in Campione is to make a personal visit and spend time talking to people. Even the real estate brokers are not particularly interested in whether or not they get your business and may not answer your letters. At the Campione end, they may not think you are serious until you arrive.

Campione is such an interesting place that a European publisher has devoted a whole book to it. *The Campione Report* is available from Scope International Ltd., Box AS125, Forestside House, Forestside, Rowlands Castle, Hants., PO9 6EE, Great Britain. The price by air courier is $125 (be sure to give a street address for delivery), or by book rate surface mail it is $100. If you'd like more information first, ask Scope for its free catalog of international reports.

CHAPTER 18

SOME
OTHER
SWISS
SECRETS

Campione isn't the only spot of soil within Swiss borders that has a unique legal status, just the most useful to the foreigner looking for Swiss loopholes. Here are two others that some readers may be able to put to use.

BUSINGEN

As is Campione, Busingen is an enclave in Switzerland. This one is German rather than Italian, and it is located just off the main highway between Zurich and the German border. Busingen is less known to international investors because it is not a tax haven, and normal German tax rates apply.

Just as with Campione, there is no physical barrier between Busingen and Switzerland. The enclave is very small and consists of a village and surrounding farmlands, with a total population of about 1,200. Since it is not a tax haven, the real estate is much cheaper than in Campione, but it has not attracted foreign residents since it offers no major advantages.

The lack of tax-haven status relative to Campione has been the main reason for this obscurity. But it is only a short commute to Zurich from Busingen, and it is relatively easy to get a German residence permit. EU citizens, of course, have an automatic right to reside in Germany. It would seem that this combination of factors is just right for somebody wanting many of the advantages of living in Switzerland but who may be unable to obtain a Swiss residency permit.

SAMNAUN

This is Switzerland's sales-tax-free shopping village, with a population of only 600. The village is exempt from normal sales taxes because at one time there was no road connecting it with Switzerland, and the only access was via Germany. A road has since been built, but the tax exemption still applies.

Gold is exempt from the Swiss sales tax anyway, but if you want to buy other precious metals (platinum, palladium, or silver) or stones (emeralds or diamonds) via the confidentiality of a Swiss bank and either take them with you or have them stored by the bank, then this is the place to do it. There are branches of Credit Suisse and the Grison Cantonal Bank in the village.

CHAPTER 19

PRIVACY TACTICS THAT CAN ENHANCE YOUR SWISS INVESTING

There are a number of little things that can help you to protect your privacy both in everyday activities and in the pursuit of offshore investing opportunities. This chapter highlights several little-known options that you may find useful.

GOLD CERTIFICATES PROVIDE PORTABLE PRIVACY

A gold certificate provides you with an attractive alternative to investing in physical metal and offers a way to transfer assets out of the country.

The Mocatta Delivery Order (MDO) is a title document representing ownership of a specific, numbered unit of gold, silver, or platinum. With origins dating back to 1671, Mocatta is the oldest bullion trading firm in the world. As one of the world's most experienced precious metals organizations, Mocatta created the MDO to satisfy the highest criteria of privacy, safety, liquidity, and flexibility.

You can choose storage in either Wilmington, Delaware, or Zurich, Switzerland. While in storage, the metal is fully insured under a Lloyds of London insurance policy.

The certificate is issued in your name (or the name of a corporation or trust, if you prefer) and identifies the physical gold, silver, or platinum owned. MDOs offer transfer-of-ownership features that enable the owner to sell, assign, or collateralize the metal easily yet ensure non-negotiability, since a lost document can be replaced, unlike a bearer security. Since the order is non-negotiable, it does not have to be reported if it is taken in or out of the United States, and there is no reporting of the purchase to the IRS. An MDO can be issued in the name of a family limited partnership or offshore trust, or it can be assigned to one of them as a means of transferring ownership of the metal when the asset-protection entity is created.

For more information on the MDO, contact:

International Financial Consultants Inc.
Suite 400A
1700 Rockville Pike
Rockville, MD 20852

USE A STAND-ALONE TELEPHONE CALLING CARD

Intended for travelers who use calling cards frequently, there is a discount telephone calling card that has a flat rate of 17.5 cents per minute for interstate calls, anytime, anywhere in the United States, including Puerto Rico, Hawaii, Alaska, and the U.S. Virgin Islands. There are no surcharges, no monthly fees, no minimum monthly billings, and international calling is also available.

The calling card is free and is a stand-alone card, meaning that a person using the card does not have to change his long-distance service. It saves up to 68 percent over the leading competitors, including prepaid phone cards (most of which are around 40 cents per minute).

But it is the "stand-alone" part that makes me mention it here. Because the card can be applied for without having to subscribe to a new long-distance service, one can use the card for things like calling overseas banks and pay the separate calling card bill from a different bank account or by money order. The record of calls made won't be showing up on your home or office phone bill, so there's no easy-to-follow trail of calls to an offshore bank or money manager. And since the separate calling card bill can be paid by money order, it doesn't create a credit card charge record, which is one of the problems in recharging prepaid phone cards. (And you don't get an embarrassing "out of time" recording and cut-off, which can easily happen when a prepaid $10 card is being used for an expensive overseas call.)

For an application form, send a stamped, addressed reply envelope to:

Center for Business Information
Attn: Phone Card Applications
816 Elm Street, Suite 187
Manchester, NH 03101-2101

HOW TO KEEP THE IRS—AND OTHER SNOOPS— OUT OF YOUR SAFE DEPOSIT BOX

A safe deposit box is a veritable necessity for keeping things like offshore bank books, precious metals certificates, bearer securities, cash, and coins. Yet a safe deposit box can create its own problems.

One obvious problem is that upon the death of the boxholder, the bank is required to deny access to the box until a properly appointed executor and an IRS agent open the box. The IRS will presume that all assets inside are the property of the deceased, so if you are holding assets there that you have given in trust to your children, they will become part of the taxable estate—or worse, they may be applied to some debt of the estate. Unreported foreign accounts could even be seized as being part of a crime. IRS agents tend to assume criminality, and you are no longer available to provide an alternative honest explanation.

But there are other safe deposit box problems that are at least as important as dealing with the box upon death. For example, if the box is in one name only, many banks will not honor a power of attorney to let somebody else have access to it in an emergency, unless the power of attorney is signed in person in the bank. If you are in a foreign hospital and need to authorize your spouse to open the box, this could become a major problem. Even if the bank will accept a notarized power of attorney, there may be problems and delays in arranging for a foreign notary to visit and then having the notary certificate authenticated by the U.S. Embassy or Consulate and sending it to the bank.

The solution is to form a corporation to hold your principal safe deposit box. The corporation can change the names of the people authorized to access the box simply by furnishing the bank with an updated resolution form. And a box belonging to a corporation is not frozen by a bank because of the death of a person, even if that person is the sole person then having access to the box.

To do this properly, I recommend that the corporation be used only to hold the safe deposit box. This provides the maximum privacy because the corporation has no activities to cause it to be audited or investigated. Under federal law, even an inactive corporation must file a tax return, but a corporate return showing no income can be filled in each year without having to pay an accountant to do it. After three years of zero-income returns, the IRS usually sends out a form letter saying there is no need to file further returns unless the corporation begins to have income.

The other obligation that must be met is to ensure that the corporation is in good standing so that you don't encounter the situation in which the corporation is deemed no longer to exist because the annual reports were not filed. Delaware is the best state for this because an inactive corporation only needs to file a simple annual return and pay an annual fee to the state (and an annual fee to its Delaware registered agent).

Privacy can be maintained by having the registered agent file the annual return with the state, signing it as "incorporator," which keeps the list of officers off the state records. Most large corporation services will not provide annual report-filing services, but the one mentioned below will do so. To be entirely safe, you can even leave funds with the registered agent to prepay the state fees each year, thus ensuring that there is no accidental termination of the corporation because of a late payment. Since the holding of a safe deposit box is not deemed to be conducting business by any state, the Delaware corporation does not need to qualify to do business in the state in which the box is held, thus improving privacy and keeping the existence of the corporation out of the public records in your own state.

For information on a service that can form a corporation for you in Delaware (or in any state), write to:

Incorporation Information Package
818 Washington Street
Wilmington, DE 19801

Keeping the IRS away is not the only reason to have a corporation hold your safe deposit box. It also keeps a personal creditor from being able to have the box frozen by a court for an inspection of the contents, which can easily happen during a lawsuit or other claim against you.

PRIVACY AND DATA ENCRYPTION

Encryption is an electronic procedure that digitally encodes (converts into unintelligible gibberish) and decodes (converts back to readable language) information. Encrypted messages can move across international borders by telephone, radio, or courier without interference. A "message" means anything that can be digitized—a sequence of words, music, a forbidden magazine or book, even a digitized picture.

Examples of everyday uses of electronic encryption include writers who send chapters of their new books to their publishers, collaborators on an invention working at a distance and needing to keep others from claim-jumping a discovery, consumers who pay bills or order from mail-order catalogs by sending encrypted credit card numbers over the telephone, accountants who scramble backup tapes so that clients needn't worry about lost confidentiality if the tapes are lost or stolen, and attorneys who communicate with clients and other attorneys via encrypted documents.

Today, any reasonably powerful desktop computer can encrypt and decrypt messages that the most powerful supercomputers in the world, working together, could not decrypt. Programs to do this are inexpensive and already available to anyone.

Most encryption programs take advantage of a mathematically sophisticated encryption technology that requires two different keys, both of which are necessary to decrypt the message. The sender needs only one to send a message. The receiver decodes the message with the second key—which never needs to leave his computer, where it can be protected by passwords. Although the mathematics are daunting, the program makes the process simple and straightforward.

It is technically feasible to use encryption to create a totally secret banking system, with account owners identities being unknown even to the bank. Credits could be transferred between accounts from anywhere in the world through encrypted communications. However, in a world where governments are increasingly subscribing to treaties limiting banking secrecy and requiring identification of depositors, it is unlikely that this scenario will actually occur in the near future. But unlikely is not impossible—and the time may come when some government permits such a service or when entrepreneurs sneak it in the back door by calling it a barter exchange instead of a bank. Since everything is electronic, such a service could even be operated from a ship, an orbiting space station, or the moon. (It is only 30 years since the first moon landing—who knows what the next 30 years might bring?) The data haven may eventually supplement the tax haven.

In the meantime, data encryption is available to individuals for whatever use they wish to make of it. A package offering basic information on encryption, including copies of several different computer programs for IBM-compatible computers, is called The Privacy Disk and is available for $49.95 from Noble Software, 51 MacDougal Street, Suite 192, New York, NY, 10012. (A 3.5" diskette will be sent unless you specify a 5.25" diskette.) Noble Software doesn't have a catalog or literature about the programs, so don't expect a reply if you write and ask for "more information" about The Privacy Disk. With the U.S. government making proposals to outlaw the sale of encryption programs, this is something you might want to buy now and put away even if you have no immediate use for it.

Privacy of electronic communications enables you to do business from anywhere in the world, with anybody in the world. And countries around the world are competing for that business. You can take advantage of what these countries have to offer to safeguard your freedom and privacy by using exactly the same techniques employed by giant multinational companies.

TAKING THE INFORMATION HIGHWAY OFFSHORE

The Internet offers a vast array of on-line services, including basic stock quotes, investment information sources, and on-line access to brokers. Whatever you're in to, the Internet offers multiple roads to get more information about it. And computers on the Internet can communicate with other "Net" computers, whether they are in the next room or on the other side of the world—without even the cost of a long-distance call.

Access to these services is as easy as dialing a phone once you have a direct Internet Access Account. It's your master key to the information wonders of cyberspace, and it provides software with *unrestricted* access to the entire Net (although many on-line services restrict you to only the services they provide, and you'll get ACCESS DENIED messages if you try to venture outside the permitted ones). This is critically important if you want to explore the world of offshore investments and banking or use the Internet to communicate with your offshore contacts.

For information on getting your own Internet Access Account, send a self-addressed stamped envelope to:

Mercury Internet Information
9 Clinton Plaza Drive, #243
Oneonta, NY 13820

ABOUT THE AUTHOR

Adam Starchild is the author of more than a dozen books and hundreds of magazine articles, primarily on international business and finance. His articles have appeared in a wide range of publications around the world, including *Business Credit, Euromoney, Finance, The Financial Planner, International Living, Offshore Financial Review, Reason, Tax Planning International, Trusts & Estates*, and many more.